THE MAKING OF A MINORITY

Political Developments in Derry and the North 1912-25

Colm Fox MA

First published in August 1997 by
Guildhall Press, 41 Great James Street,
L'Derry, Northern Ireland BT48 7DF
Tel: (01504) 364413 Fax: (01504) 372949

© Colm Fox/Guildhall Press 1997

ISBN 0 946451 40 0

Guildhall Press receives support from the Training & Employment Agency under the
Action for Community Employment scheme.

Cover photograph courtesy William Clifford Collection
Typeset and designed by Joe Mc Allister

Special thanks to Manus Martin (T&EA), and Derry City Council's Recreation and Leisure
Department for generous Community Services Grant Aid.

Acknowledgements

I wish to record my appreciation for the assistance and patience of Dr Gerry O'Brien (Magee College). I am also grateful for the advice and courtesy of the staff at Magee College Library, Central Libray in Derry and Public Records Office, Belfast. I received practical advice and encouragement from Maureen my wife and from Maura my daughter. Patrick and Paul also gave practical help and amused encouragement when necessary.

I would also like to record my thanks to the following: Dr Eamon Phoenix for helpful insights, P J Doherty, Anton McCabe, Mr Leo Emerson, Moya Jane O'Doherty, Dr Mary Leary and Ken Ward. Also to Magee College, the Bigger-McDonald Collection and the William Clifford Collection for the use of their photographs.

CONTENTS

FOREWORD BY JOHN HUME

The period 1912-25 must rank among the most dramatic and traumatic phases of Irish history. On some levels its history is fascinating, on so many others it is frustrating. This comes through very clearly in this study by Colm Fox which explores the experience of Derry City in the context of the political agitations and machinations of the time.

The study's scope is not strictly confined to 1912-25, it rightly takes good account of contributory and background factors. It also has relevance for our current circumstances as many of the fears, grievances and suspicions which inform our political divisions are evident, if not sourced, in that period.

Tracing the history of a city against the background of the events which involved or affected the whole country proves, in this study, to illuminate the reader's understanding of both local and national history and the relationship between the two.

The impact of the developments of the time on Derry is strongly traced and Colm Fox shows how those experiences indelibly influenced political attitudes in the city. His study explores how the creation of Northern Ireland sentenced the city of Derry to become an affront to democracy through sectarian gerrymandering and a gross example of injustice in civic policy and public services, realising the fears of Derry's Nationalists at the time of partition.

This outstanding study is clearly written from a Nationalist perspective. That does not make it a partial study of the issues and events which the author chose to examine. Equally its Derry focus does not make it a parochial study or involve a loss of perspective on wider events. It will prove to be of value and interest not just to Derry people and not just to Nationalists. If anyone wants to improve their understanding of northern Nationalist perceptions they will find this book insightful.

Such insight in itself would make the book worthwhile. But the inescapable resonances between events then and now give it an even more profound relevance. We can all learn today from work like this which offer a clearer understanding of another period of serious mistakes in Irish history.

INTRODUCTION

The purpose of this study is to examine the events and influences which contributed to the Nationalist majority of Derry City's population being converted to an electoral minority. It will look at the general and the specific factors involved. One main theme will be to analyse the factors and events that resulted in what Nationalists saw as their abandonment by the Provisional Free State Government and the English Liberals.

The study will also look at the change in Derry's relative position from one of pivotal importance in the political equilibrium of nine-county Ulster, to its relegation to the periphery of Northern Ireland, politically and economically.

While the specific area of study is 1912-25 it is essential to strive to detect those earlier trends and influences in the nineteenth century and how they eventually impacted upon the Nationalists of the North. In this respect the role of the Catholic Church and the rise of cultural Nationalism with its effect on the two traditions of Irish Nationalism, the revolutionary and the constitutional, will also be explored.

Direct attention will be given to the significant events of 1912-25, the founding of the UVF, the Irish Volunteers, the 1916 Rising, the Anglo-Irish War, the Treaty and the Civil War, and how they influenced the ultimate partition of Ireland. This study will also attempt to trace the origin of partition as an issue, and its ruinously divisive effect on Northern Nationalists, precisely at a time when a cohesive stance was imperative in gaining them a more secure future. At all stages, the study will endeavour to show how the impact of events in general affected or influenced the politics and ambitions of Derry Nationalists.

CHAPTER ONE

THE ORIGINS OF TWO TRADITIONS

Doire Calgach, Doire Colmcille were ancient settlements on the site of the present walled city. There may be doubt about who founded the first religious settlement but few would disagree that it became famous as a religious settlement of Columba, the kinsman of the O'Donnell and the O'Neill.[1] It was used, through the founding of its sister abbey in Iona, as a launching point for the Christianisation of Scotland and Northern England. With the founding of Lindisfarne by Aidan and disciples of Columba the Columban mission was to extend into Europe restoring christianity and love of classical learning to Dark Ages Europe. Derry and Iona acted as universities for the princes of Europe because distant Christian Ireland was the repository of classical and Christian learning in an almost totally vandalized Europe. This tradition survived into the late middle ages when sadly the gradual deterioration began until the sparsely populated ruins of monasteries and churches met the gaze of the first English settlers in the middle of the sixteenth century.[2]

The successful building of a walled city in 1614 under the auspices of the London Companies, known as the Irish Society, meant that Derry, while still a small colonial outpost, was to be crucial in the Williamite Wars of 1689-90, and therefore in British and European history. Here was to start the second tradition which was to be the source of historical myth and Protestant symbolism to rival that of the Saints and Scholars. In sustaining a heroic siege, on the winning side, Derry was to become the holy city of Protestant obduracy. Like all myths it took time to evolve, and was not fully to mature in all its lurid symbolism until it was to be needed to repel another

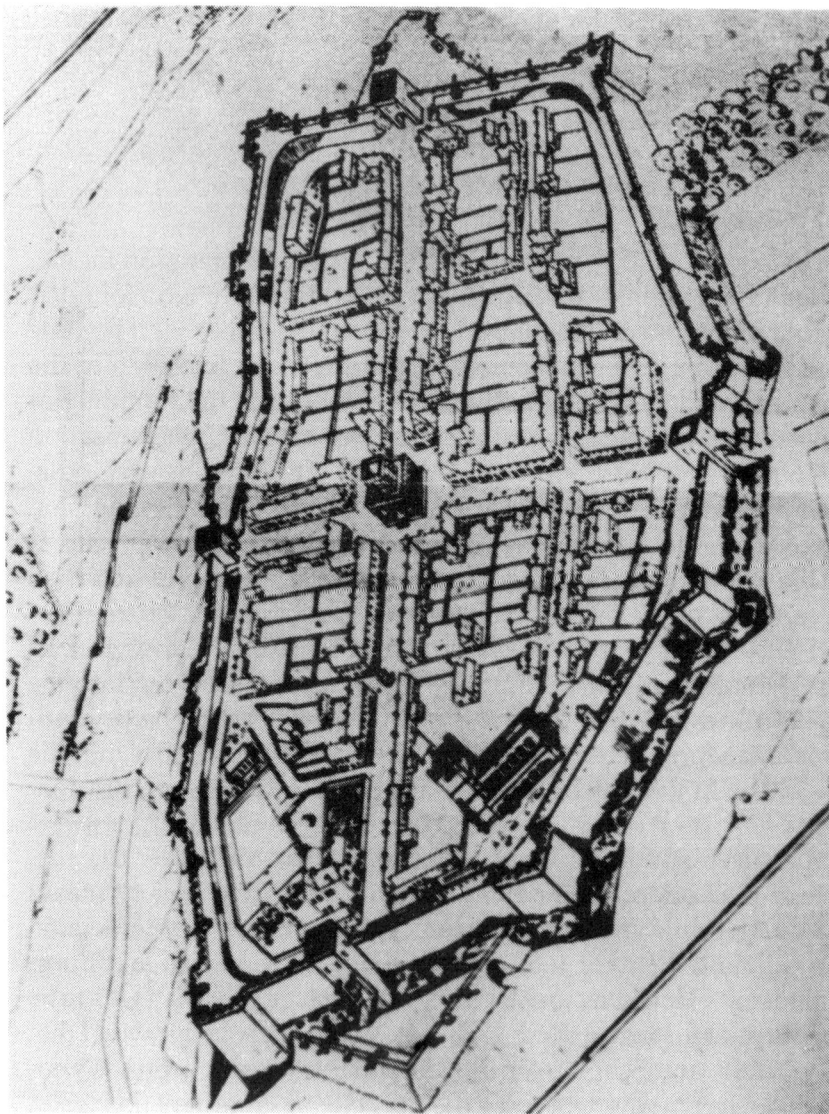

Map of Derry, 1689, at the time of the Great Siege. *(Photograph: Magee College)*

apparent threat, when the enemy at the gate were the city's expanding population with their consequent politicisation in the Home Rule campaign. Thus was to begin in Irish politics, the "siege mentality" which the Protestants viewed as a heroic precedent, but others saw as a retreat into the citadel of parochial materialism and identity crisis. The closest modern example was that of the Afrikaaners with their "laager mentality" perpetually insecure in a hostile environment, while their rootless culture atrophied into a neurotic defensiveness. The first centennial of the siege was celebrated in what from present-day experience would have been seen as a decorous affair with a stately municipal procession, involving, (strange to modern eyes), Catholic clergy.[3] It was very obviously lacking the sectarian abrasiveness that the nervous insecure Protestant citizens of the nineteenth century indulged in. However the siege was to be crucial in formulating an identity and forming attitudes in northern Protestants.

Derry or Londonderry was to sink into relative obscurity, being eventually dethroned from its Ulster primacy by the rapid nineteenth century industrial development of Belfast. This was more a part of the expansion of southern Scottish and northern English industrialisation than a development of Irish economy.[4] Belfast benefitted from cheap raw materials of imperial origin and easy entry into the ready markets of the empire. These factors were to weigh heavily with the northern Unionists in their opposition to Home Rule. Belfast was not so much the capital of Ulster, or the industrial capital of Ireland, as an integral part of British industrialisation.[5] Derry too developed industrially and rapidly urbanized but at a relatively slower rate than Belfast.

Derry appeared again in a pivotal role politically in the late nineteenth and early twentieth century. The Londonderry Westminster seat was crucial in deciding the balance of power in the thirty-three Ulster seats almost evenly divided between Nationalist and Conservative-Unionist. Parnell was reputed to have said that 'he would rather hold Derry than hold forty seats.'[6] The effect of the close-fought nature of the political rivalry will later be examined for its implications in Derry itself.

In the late eighteenth century, events were unfolding throughout Europe and Britain, which were to have a sequel in Derry as distinct from other parts of Ireland. It is necessary to look briefly at those influences working at a profound level which were to produce, from 1885 on, the strong Nationalist momentum and its Unionist reaction that were to shape the future fate of Derry City. This is the city which in the Westminister election of 1918 was to return a revolutionary Nationalist (Sinn Féin) member but within three years was to be forcibly locked into a repressive one-party Unionist statelet, overtly hostile to all that the majority of its citizens stood for.

The multiplicity of forces at work included in the main constitutional Nationalism, revolutionary Nationalism, the role of the church, the various strands of Unionism and, of course, the part played by the British Government in Ireland, in its aspect as a Unionist force in the Anglo-Irish situation.

In looking at Nationalism anywhere in modern Europe, it has to be conceded that the seminal influence of the French Revolution was to stimulate the formation of many Nationalisms, springing from the cultural and socio-economic needs of developing nations. With the industrial revolution and the emergence of a new industrial bourgeoisie there was a great momentum for modernization. The fact that the industrial expansion in Ireland was not evenly distributed but was virtually confined to the north-east corner of the island was to have significant implications in the twentieth century. The effect, direct or indirect, of this revolutionary Nationalism was to reverberate down two centuries to have a profound influence in the shaping of modern Ireland. These effects on Ireland were twofold, the direct one being the involvement of the revolutionary French army here in 1798, perhaps never a determined one, and the indirect ideological influences, of a much longer duration.

The liberation and "sovereignty of the people" ideology of the French revolution was always going to appeal to the northern Presbyterians with their own anti-establishment traditions of democracy, more so under the penal and exclusive rule of the Episcopalians at the end of the eighteenth century. While the '98 rebellion failed, the spirit of militant republicanism was to become an Irish political undercurrent, sporadically emerging on centre stage in 1848 and 1867, before its ultimate manifestation in the 1916 Rising and its aftermath.

The other form of Nationalism, usually referred to as constitutional was of a persuasive and reformist nature, though not beyond making political capital out of physical resistance and intimidation when it suited. Full political and cultural Nationalism did not emerge in Ireland until the end of the nineteenth century. Its embryonic stages were a type of grievance politics, relating to Catholic Emancipation, nurtured by the highly skillful Daniel O'Connell into the more political Nationalist Repeal movement. Widespread and deeply felt agitation on the land question, in the post Famine era, was, by its success, to culminate in the creation of the Irish Party furthering the cause of Home Rule.

The unifying effect of Nationalism was also helped in Ireland as elsewhere by the expansion of the railways and the introduction of compulsory schooling with its consequent spread of literacy and the availability of more newspapers, books and libraries. Within this modernizing process a motivated middle class participated, as teachers, writers, journalists, poets, driven to invent or recreate an inclusive sense of cultural identity. This type of cultural Nationalism was stimulating, emancipatory, and above all invited everyone to participate; at core it dangled the prize of liberty and democracy. Some see the European upsurge of Nationalism and socialism, as a substitute for comforting religions, displaced by the massive social and economic dislocation of the industrial revolution. Thus the myth-maker went to work. Yeats, Synge, Lady Gregory and Standish O Grady created an idyllic Celtic past, with, of course its epic heroes like Cuchulainn. Ireland's past was excavated to exploit its raw material for the myth creators. Interest in the Gaelic language was revived by Douglas Hyde and Eoin McNeill, who was personally to play a role in Derry's future fate. There was a ferment of activity involving literature, drama, economics, art and language. Similar cultural movements had been taking place in Europe, with attendant myth making and symbol creating processes. Mazzini with his Young Europe and Risorgimento Nationalism, which so influenced Young Irelanders, was to call on the great Roman classical past to be later given more sinister overtones by Mussolini. The German Nationalists invoked the spirits of the Teutonic Knights to be revered in music and literature. New symbols of Nationalism to replace those of the *ancien regime* were fashioned in Ireland, the

17

harp, the shamrock, the round tower, the wolfhound, and Kathleen Ni Houlihan.

It is worth noting that while Catholicism was part of the unifying force of Nationalism in Ireland, the most active and ardent of the Irish myth creators were Protestant, possibly a cultural response to the Protestant identity crisis, created by a century of cumulative Nationalist/Catholic pressure. Whatever, this was to show significantly, along with the Presbyterian role in early Republicanism, that despite appearances, Irish Nationalism was not sectarian. This, however, is the very point that was to prove critical in the North where siege mentality Protestants did not respond with reciprocal tolerance and this was to be an essential factor in the creation of partition.

Mazzini, in compounding a sense of nationhood, pointed to language, as an important common heritage indicator, and listed eleven nations that conformed to his comprehensive criteria. He omitted Ireland on the grounds that a native language was not commonly extant there.[7] While he was not entirely right in dismissing the validity of Irish Nationalism, he certainly pinpointed what was to be a matter of self-conscious difficulty for Nationalist purists from the Gaelic League through De Valera to the present day.

With the progressive settlements and colonization of the Protestant Tudors and their descendants, resulting in the death of the native language, the most distinctive difference between planter and gael became religion. This was to have a particular bearing on the politics of the North, the most Protestant province in Ireland. It was also to highlight the role of the Catholic Church in the progressively political national movements of the nineteenth century. This role was further strengthened with the easing of the penal laws, Catholic emancipation, and the devotional revolution of the nineteenth century. The church leaders role will be shown to be particularly significant in the North at a critical time affecting partition, and crucially in Derry City regarding the isolation of Derry Nationalists from the political mainstream.

With the arrival of Archbishop Cullen to Armagh in 1850, a liturgical, devotional and administrative revival of the Catholic Church in Ireland began. This was largely the Romanising of the church so that it became less the Irish Catholic Church, and more the Universal Catholic Church in Ireland. As the ex-rector of the Irish College in Rome, he shared the continental clerics' horror of revolution after 1848 and so strongly disapproved of the Young Irelanders and the Fenians.[8] Bishop Kelly of Derry was to follow the devotional route, by building a new cathedral, St Eugene's and inviting to his diocese various religious orders such as the Christian Brothers and Sisters of Mercy. The huge cathedral, dominating the Derry skyline was to reflect the new found Catholic confidence of an emerging, though small, Catholic middle class which was to influence the development of Derry Nationalist politics well into the twentieth century.[9] Bishop Kelly remained hostile to Nationalist politics in general though elsewhere church leaders like Archbishop Croke took a different line.

However the Home Rule Party under Parnell had been so effective in exploiting the balance of power in Westminster politics and mobilizing mass support from the largely successful land war that the Catholic church leaders were dragged reluctantly in his wake. This is a factor referred to by Sean O'Faoilin in his book *The Irish* where he relates the possibly apocryphal story of the socialist leaders of the Paris 1848 revolution who were seen to be walking behind the mob. When asked why they were not at the front of the mob leading, they replied, that in that position they would be unable to see where the mob was going. In other words the Catholic church for all its alleged dominance quietly acquiesced in the presence of a determined middle class. Its dominance therefore came not from inherent strength so much as good timing and judgment. Also, with controversial matters, the church could always be seen to be on the winning side, by having clerics on both sides.

The manner of Parnell's downfall was to reverberate into the politics of Derry in a particularly unfortunate way. The reaction of the Church in general, and the Derry clergy in particular to the divorce case was to assert their moral leadership in the political field.[10] Where before the church deferred to the Irish Parliamentary Party, they now regained a position of dominance amongst the national population, which was also to expose their political limitations at local level. The post-Parnell phase of internecine strife ended around the turn of the century with Redmond and Joe Devlin uniting the party as the United Irish League. Still fearing the divisiveness of Nationalist politics, the Derry clergy deterred the United Irish League from recruiting or canvassing in Derry so pulling the city away from the broad stream of Irish Nationalist politics.[11]

During this period of political dysfunction for Derry Catholics the Derry Unionists did not to miss the opportunity, and so sponsored the hideously misnamed Londonderry Improvement Bill in 1895.[12] From 1851 Catholics had been in the majority but had limited municipal franchise. This was due to the fact that there were few Catholic property owners and a high disenfranchised female proportion of their population which had been attracted to the city's shirt factories. By the 1890s the city had experienced a much more rapid increase of population (mainly Nationalist) and geographical expansion, thereby threatening the Unionist dominance. The Londonderry Improvement Bill was enacted at Westminister with very little let or hindrance from the Nationalist MPs distracted by their internal factionalism. This contrasted with the Irish Parliamentary Party's protective attitude to the Catholic minority of Belfast.[13] So the Unionists succeeded in manipulating the wards and boundaries in their favour, the first quasi-legal gerrymander of many which municipal governance in Derry City was to experience.

The Protestant control of Derry City had been uncontested up to the mid-nineteenth century. They were subject as elsewhere in the North of Ireland to tension between the Church of Ireland and Presbyterianism, with the latter broadly backing liberals and the former the Tories. It was the Tories who influenced the previously neutral Apprentice Boys to become more sectarian, and flamboyantly provocative. The Derry Presbyterians supported the Tenant Right movement, so giving rise to a Presbyterian newspaper *The Derry Standard*. *The Standard* had a very forthright editor, McKnight who under the banner of "Tenant Right, Live and Let Live" sallied forth to attack establishment positions. The Protestants alternated between supporting Tory and Liberal MPs for Derry until the issue of the Land Acts and Home Rule concentrated their thinking and prompted their part in the formation of the Ulster Unionist Council 1905, and the strong revival of the Orange Order. This reaction in the North appeared to induce a partitionist element in their thinking whether conscious or not as the UUC, was almost geographically defined. After Walter Long and James Craig they eventually chose as their leader in 1911 the Dublin lawyer Edward Carson who had so ruthlessly implemented "Bloody Balfour's" policies in the land war. These repressive policies alternating with more liberal land legislation were documented as "killing Home Rule with kindness".

Historically the position of the British Government was to vary in its attitude to Ireland. This ranged from virtual genocide, plantation with a view to "civilization", integration (Act of Union), to neglect, but never carried out with any great resolution. It is arguable that continued resistance of one sort or another, political, revolutionary or both was a response to this irresolute approach. This was surely true in the case of Nationalists and figured largely in the reactions of the Ulster Unionists from 1912 on. Had the Liberals prosecuted their case for Home Rule more incisively from 1885 onwards while the Unionists were in relative disarray and unarmed, some form of acceptable resolution could have been arrived at. As it was Gladstone envisaged a Home Rule based loosely on Grattan's Parliament of Protestant gentry and could not fully comprehend how the Land Acts and Franchise Acts were to change the political face of Ireland in a way that was threatening to Unionists. It was a mistake not to include some provision for Ulster Unionists in the first Home Rule Bills. The Conservatives were to identify with Unionism for reasons partly of an imperialist nature, but mainly for internal British political reasons. Bonar Law was later to say 'it was the certainty of British support which created the strength of Ulster resistance.'[15] These elements outlined above, in British policy, both Conservative and Liberal, allied to the pragmatic acceptance by the Dublin provisional Government of Northern intransigence were important contributory factors to partition

The land question loomed large in the development of Home Rule and Irish Nationalism generally. This gave rise to an impassioned sense of justice and determined successful agitation which were to give a new confidence and assertiveness to rural Irish masses. This was not so in the North. Due to the type of Ulster settlement there was much less abrasiveness between tenants and landlords.

St Columba's Day, 9 June 1898, Long Tower. *(Photograph: William Clifford Collection)*

Certainly the rural Presbyterian tenants were not always happy with the "Ulster Custom", in land holdings as it was called. The Ulster Custom gave the tenant a reasonable expectation of holding land so long as rent was paid and allowed him to sell this right of holding to anyone acceptable to the landlord. However this was a custom and not a law, so that in certain circumstances tenants began to suffer the same pressures as their Southern counterparts from high rents and evictions, though never as widespread and ruthless. In 1847, Sharman Crawford the Ulster born MP for Rochdale tried to legalise the Ulster Custom in Westminster but was defeated.[15] This underlined the vulnerability of Ulster farmers and gave rise to the widespread Tenant Right agitation which had the support of the Presbyterian Churches. However the intensity of the campagin and the mobilisation of the masses in North-West Ulster were of a minor order compared to the west and south, and did not have the physical force undertones. The north west of Ulster, did though, feel the political fall-out from the campaign on both Nationalist and Unionist sides.

It has already been observed how the Derry clergy exploited the Nationalist confusion after the fall of Parnell. Their strong influences was to be felt in other ways. This particularly tense period was to coincide with the presence in the Long Tower parish of a greatly revered and locally influential cleric, Fr Willie Doherty, who virtually single handedly, in tune with the myth makers in Dublin, and the West, helped to re-create the potent symbolism of the Columban settlement in Doire Colmcille.[17] The occasion was the thirteen hundredth anniversary of the birth of St Columba. Father Doherty published a book which pinpointed the exact locations of the original ancient monastic settlement, restored an ancient "holy well" of Columban origin, created new Columban devotions for every 9 June, and introduced the wearing of emblematic oak leaves in honour of Columba. He indicated his own Church, the Long Tower, as having a historical connection with the original Dubh Regles though some of this was later to be disputed.[18] This was to reinforce the local sense of Catholic and Nationalist identity and was to be a symbolic counterbalance to the Protestant myth of the siege.[19] Derry was now a City with two competing traditions.

Another way the local clergy were to assert their authority was, strangely enough, in the matter of sport. Until the 1880s Catholic clergy had encouraged participation in Gaelic Athletic Association. sports along general Nationalist lines. When it emerged that the Irish Republican Brotherhood were having an undue influence on the GAA giving it a militant Republican tone, and were to take a pro-Parnell line after 1891, the Derry clergy dissuaded the local youth away from its influences.[20] They encouraged them to play soccer and later they formed the City's first professional team Derry Celtic. That soccer tradition was to endure to the present day making Derry one of the most important soccer towns in Ireland.

Local clergy's attitude was characterized by an anti-Republican view, continuing the tradition of Cardinal Cullen and Bishop Kelly. The clergy thus vehemently opposed all attempts by Sinn Féin to recruit in the town in the early 1900s. Thus with their clergy's negative attitude to the newly formed UIL (which they believed would be divisive among Derry Nationalists) and the Republican tendency, Derry Nationalist became isolated from the mainstream of Nationalist politics to 1914.[21]

As already mentioned, the close fought nature of Derry's Westminster seat was to have political implications; it discouraged extremists, or division on either side as this could split the vote. This intense partisanship is understandable, in view of the single or double figure majorities in which the contests were wont to result. Derry was usually the pivotal seat in deciding the Ulster majority or minority in thirty-three seats. Great significance in the Derry electoral area impinged upon the registration of voters and post election appeals. Derry was thus notable for very high polls, usually one of the highest in the British Isles, returning famously on one occasion (1910) 101% of the electorate.[22]

By the time we arrive at 1912, various trends had contrived at the isolation of Derry Nationalists from the mainstream of Irish Nationalist politics. There was a dominant Catholic clergy (in the absence of a strong Catholic middle-class) who had exploited the internal strife of post-Parnell Nationalism. Also influential was the clergy's successful rejection of the GAA, Sinn Féin, and the undercurrent of militant Republicanism that they threatened. It should

24

be emphasized that the clergy were not against violence *per se*, but in moral terms, maintaining that it should only be used if it had a fair chance of succeeding. No doubt they were also conscious that violence could be met with repression,and the potential loss of constitutional gains, important to the Catholic church in the nineteenth century. However, it is also noted that revolutionary Republicanism implied a type of secularism that threatened the strong authority of the church in all social matters. Another factor affecting Derry Nationalists, was the timely but effective myth making symbolism of St Columba on his thirteen hundredth anniversary which was to afford a potent counterweight to Unionist symbolism. There was also the close-fought nature of Derry elections which deterred extremism, making it appear indulgent and dangerously divisive. Derry Nationalists were not directly involved with the land question, with a relatively peaceful hinterland favoured by the Ulster Custom, so they did not feel that confidence of political achievement experienced by southern Nationalists, but they were to benefit from its fruits. The last serious riots in Derry had been in 1883, when Catholics rioted for a week after a Nationalist parade was fired at in the Diamond. Therefore Derry Catholics while still harbouring frustration at their gerrymandered corporation and maintaining deep Nationalist aspirations were reasonably quiescent under the guidance of a confident and protective clergy, as they approached the momentous events that were to begin in 1912.

CHAPTER TWO

DERRY'S PART IN IRELAND'S "PHONY" WAR
1912-14

The balance of power at Westminster was now with the reunited Irish Parliamentary Party (also called the United Irish League) and so another Home Rule Bill was inevitable. With the formation of the Ulster Unionist Council in 1905 as a reaction to the threat of Home Rule and the formation of Sinn Féin in that same year, the lines for future confrontation were already being drawn. The selection by Ulster Protestants of Edward Carson as their leader was to be very significant. Carson, a Dublin barrister and aide to Balfour when he was Chief Secretary of Ireland, was to personify Unionist defiance to Home Rule.

In Derry the 1910 election had been narrowly lost to the Tories, with Shane Leslie representing Nationalist interests. This cousin of Winston Churchill had been recommended to the newly ordained Dr McHugh, Bishop of Derry by Bishop O'Donnell of Raphoe who was to prove an influential and more perceptive figure in northern Nationalism.[1] The clerical influence on Nationalist politics since the death of Parnell had reduced Derry to a backwater in relation to national issues. So lax had interest in politics become, with consecutive Nationalist losses, that the popular Fr Willie Doherty had called a convention of all local Nationalist people in 1906 to review their parlous political state. Its main recommendation was the re-employment of Michael McDaid, a knowledgeable veteran of Derry's registration war, as election agent. Some political vigour returned and resulted in the close run contest of 1910.[2]

Though Carson championed the Ulster Unionist cause, he probably did so in the belief that he could use Ulster resistance to make

27

Home Rule impossible for any part of Ireland.[3] When the motives of his fellow Ulster Unionists were eventually revealed Carson was to be cruelly disillusioned. Under Carson's urging the Ulster Covenant was signed in 1912 and a new force, the Ulster Volunteer Force, formed in January 1913 under the command of Lt General Sir George Richardson, to oppose the impending Home Rule Bill. This treasonous policy was openly led and supported by the ex-Solicitor-General of Ireland, Carson.

By this stage the idea of partition, in one form or another, had already been mooted. A T Q Stewart quotes Lord Macauley, in reply to Daniel O'Connell's Repeal demands, suggesting some form of partition, with a legislature in Dublin and one in Derry or in some other large northern town.[4] The first detailed proposal in response to threats from Ulster Protestants came from Liberal MP T S Agar-Roberts, who suggested the exclusion of the four Protestant counties, Antrim, Down, Derry and Armagh.[5] This suggestion was supported by Carson on the grounds that a four county statelet would quickly collapse, thus wrecking Home Rule, which was always Carson's goal, rather than partition. Churchill had also warned Redmond in 1912 that he might advocate some form of temporary exclusion.[6] The Liberals were already losing determination in the face of Unionist and Conservative opposition. Asquith mentioned partition as a possibility to the King on 6 February 1912, if there was fresh pressure of opinion requiring special treatment for the Ulster counties.[7]

By 1913 it was beginning to become apparent that the prize of Home Rule might be tainted for northern Nationalists, and impossible for Ulster Unionists. With the death of the Duke of Abercorn an election was called in Derry which was to reveal the lack of preparedness of the Nationalists in the city to confront the impending dramatic events. The Nationalists had made some form of recovery, as already mentioned due to the intervention of Fr Willie Doherty, but due to their continued isolation from mainstream national politics and with local clergy in the shape of Bishop McHugh suspiciously guarding their influence , they were once more without a candidate. With no political parties operating as such, funding elections was a problem. The Bishop had to find someone of independent means as a last desperate approach to Redmond in Dublin had failed. He persuaded Mr David Hogg, a local Presbyterian factory owner, who in 1880s had been a Liberal and former Home Ruler, but such was the current atmosphere in Ulster, that he managed to complete the campaign, and narrowly win the seat by 27 votes without making any committment to Home Rule.[8] Crucially this win gave the Nationalists a 17-16 majority in the nine Ulster counties. The almost complete clerical control of Derry Nationalist politics, sustained in isolation from 1891-1913, was to be radically challenged in the early months of 1914.

This challenge was to be brought about by a man who was to strongly influence Derry's move to a more militant Nationalism but who was, ironically, also to be identified with the final defeat of its Nationalist aspirations. John McNeill as he was usually known in the North, was a Glensman who came from Glenarm. As a bright university student at St Malachy's Belfast he won one of the hotly-competed places in the civil service in Dublin. While studying in St Malachy's he had heard the unforgettable fracas of the sectarian riots following the first Home Rule Bill. He went on with Douglas Hyde to found the Gaelic League in 1890 and later became professor of Early Irish History at UCD. He subsequently changed his name to Eoin and it was thus he became known throughout Ireland. After the formation of the Ulster Volunteer Force in 1913, MacNeill published an article in *An Claidheamh Soluis* (Sword of Light) on 1 November 1913, "The North Began" in which he commended the example of the Ulster Unionists, as showing they were 'masters of their own fate.' This article advocating physical resistance had even more impact coming from a well-known political moderate, a follower of Redmond. It only remained for the southern Nationalists to do the same, as the British Government was now obviously acquiescing to the recruiting and drilling of volunteers. MacNeill was afterwards approached by Bulmer Hobson, an IRB man, and the O'Rahilly to take the matter further and on 25 November 1913 at a massive public rally at the Rotunda Rink in Dublin the Irish Volunteers were formed.

Initially they were ignored by wealthy Nationalists and the UIL, who felt that they threatened the Home Rule Bill then going through the Commons. In the judgement of the Inspector General of the Royal Irish Constabulary 'the new force (Irish Volunteers) is not likely to be formidable.'[9] The spread of the Irish Volunteers was rapid and in a few months, by March, they were openly drilling in seventeen counties. On the first of May they had one-hundred-and-ninety-one branches, and over 25,000 members.[10] The inspector-general (RIC) estimated the UVF in March to number 84,000 (not 100,000 as newspaper reported) and well equipped with 25,000 rifles, they had also stopped recruiting.[11] In Derry the first Irish Volunteer groups were formed in February and began to organize and drill under the command of Charles O'Neill DL and Alderman Patrick Campbell. Originally mainly working-class men had been attracted but within a few months all classes joined, with the support of the clergy, and the endorsement of Redmond and Devlin.[12]

The Volunteers in Derry had, in an excess of new-found enthusiasm and confidence, arranged a monster rally and march to Celtic Park for 14 February. This was beginning to alarm the Derry Unionists and UVF unused to militant opposition from Derry Nationalists in the previous twenty-five years. The Bishop was requested by an increasingly nervous Redmond to ban the march lest any resultant violence would interfere with his delicate neogotiations with the Liberals.[13] This he reluctantly did, though this reluctance was tinged with a realistic acceptance that he was now being confronted by forces beyond his control, a new found vigorous Nationalism in Derry, and a mercurial political climate in the country at large. The Derry Volunteers arranged another route-march for mid-March in defiance of his Lordship, and were restrained only by pleas from Redmond and by hell and brimstone denouncements from the altar.[14] The whole atmosphere generated throughout Ireland by Carson, the UVF and the Irish Volunteers was creating a new political ambience. It was becoming clear to the clergy and the leaders of the UIL that this movement was becoming irresistible and that they themselves would need to be involved, which they duly became in June, when recruitment soared from 28,000 to 69,000.[15] Even in April 1914 Derry City had battalions in the Bogside, the United Irish League Hall, Rosemount, Waterside and Bishop Street. The first battalion the 1st Derry Regiment, with its headquarters in the Shamrock

Commander James McGlinchey of the 1st Derry Regiment of the Irish
Volunteers, in Celtic Park 1914. *(Photograph: Magee College)*

Hall, Bogside, was the strongest, having eight companies and close on one thousand members. Under the command of Mr James McGlinchey they had attained great proficiency in drill. After the postponed marches and growth of the IV the Bishop and clergy feared more open defiance and set up a committee of local dignatories including some priests and selected as leader of the Derry Irish Volunteers another intriguing character, as colourful as he was contradictory, Captain J R White. Though his contribution was of a transient nature he was to be one of the memorable characters to emerge from an era of turmoil and change.

Captain J R White, DSO was a distinguished veteran of the Boer War. He was the son of Field Marshal Sir George White, the hero of Ladysmith, and on retiring from the army he had arrived in Ulster, where he became, not surprisingly, confused by the motives of the Unionists, who were threatening to fight the British Army in order to remain British. On arrival in Dublin he sympathised with the locked out strikers being starved into submission and being physically assaulted by the police. He suggested to Connolly that he would train groups of strikers as a defensive force to protect pickets and meetings from police attack.[16] On 13 November 1913, this scion of an upper class military family sat on the platform with James Connolly, the marxist trade Unionist, who declaimed to a great rally 'I am going to talk sedition' and proceeded to go along with White's suggestion and proposed the setting up of 'battalions of trained men.' He was flanked by the formidable Countess Markievicz, another apparent aristocratic contradiction and together they witnessed that night the birth of the Irish Citizen Army which was to play such a significant role in the 1916 Rising and the future history of Ireland. White was to go on to become chairman of a reorganised Army Council when the original ICA dwindled away with the end of the strike in February 1914. White clashed with Larkin over a plan to affiliate with the Irish Volunteers and he and Sean O'Casey drifted away, with White turning up in Derry in April.[18]

He duly commanded the Derry Volunteers though in a manner that was to cause problems. He was not always sensitive to local feelings, and local inexperience in matters military, though all his NCO's were ex-service men. He was involved in a local misunderstanding with the UVF, which was to have its humorous side. The by now numerous and active Derry Irish Volunteers had arranged a route-march for one of its battalions, roughly 400 men accompanied by their band, which proceeded in the direction of Molenan, 3 miles from the City. There they began to drill in a field near to the residence of Captain Moore, who happened to be the leader of the local UVF. He, fearing an attack, sounded the alarm and mobilised two hundred of his regiment and set up armed sentries guarding his house. The Irish Volunteers reacted to this by sending into Derry for reinforcements, and a strong party started off. The police, however, were able to advise Captain White of these events, and he promptly drove off in pursuit, turned the men back, and ordered the battalion at Molenan not to interfere with Captain Moore or his men. Thus ended the great Molenan stand-off.[19]

From April the Derry Irish Volunteers drilled nightly in Celtic Park, and also on Sundays, drawing large crowds of admiring sympathisers. The effect on the UVF was to confine them to their drill halls where they protected their weapons from expected attack. The RIC County Inspector Carey, when he regarded the local Irish Volunteers 'as a formidable association and a cause of unrest among the citizens,' would appear to have been referring mainly to Unionist citizens. On 16 June 1914, the Irish Volunteers called a mobilisation and remained on the streets until 2.00am.[20] What can be deduced from local reports, including RIC reports, is the emergence of a new assertiveness and confidence amongst the Nationalist people, that they were once more beginning to participate effectively in national politics.

The police were concerned about potential conflict between the Irish Volunteers and the UVF, though from their own reports the UVF were making strenuous efforts to avoid such a contingency. This was after the Larne gun-running, during which the RIC reported that 1,600 rifles were brought into Derry.[21] They assessed the Irish Volunteers as having a good supply of revolvers but very few rifles.

Partition now appeared openly as an issue with the Asquith Government's indecision being exploited by Carson and Bonar Law, who now threatened armed uprising and the suborning of the Brit-

"B" Company 2nd Battalion City of Derry Regiment UVF, January 1915. *(Photograph: McDonald-Bigger Collection)*

ish Army. Asquith transferred the threatening pressure of Carson and Bonar Law to Redmond, convincing him that if he did not concede some sort of partition, even of a temporary nature, (six years), Conservatives would force a general election which the Liberals would lose, and Home Rule would be shelved. This concession by Redmond marked the beginning of the serious decline of the Irish Party. Redmond made frantic efforts to assure Bishop McHugh that he could guarantee a Derry City 'opt out' from exclusion (ie by plebiscite) which temporarily mollified the uneasy Bishop. Events were at fever pitch. *The Derry Journal* reported Churchill's speech at Bradford on 14 March during which he castigated Carson as 'indulging in a treasonable conspiracy' and ended with a rousing challenge to: 'Let us go forward together and put these grave matters to the proof.'[22] The reaction of *The Times of London* to the possible Derry City opt-out was to reflect the utterly reckless disregard at the highest levels for parliamentary democracy that now obtained in the home of Mother of Parliaments. *The Times* began by attributing any prosperity Derry had to the work of Unionists, ignoring the fact the current Derry MP was David Hogg, shirt manufacturer and Home Ruler. It went on to say:

> It is unthinkable that Londonderry which never surrendered to the force of arms, *will passively surrender now to a few votes in a ballot box**. In any case we are perfectly certain that Protestant Ulster will never yield up the City of the Siege, and that Londonderry presents a quite insuperable obstacle to the new proposals in their present form.
>
> *Author's italics

It can be seen here how readily the old mythic symbolism could be exploited in defence of Tory political advantage, no matter what a 'few votes in a ballot box' might represent. The deliberate dismissal of democracy by this journalistic organ of the British establishment was strengthening the case of the physical force parties in Ireland. They could now show that constitiutional methods were ineffectual against gun runners and armed traitors threatening democracy, though the nature of British democracy itself has not always been unquestionable. Thus news of the Larne gun-running in April 1914 was to lead to a surge of membership in the Irish Volunteers.

When the Liberals and reluctant Redmondites proposed the Home Rule Bill on 9 March 1914, it was rejected outright by Carson. But Churchill's Bradford speech and clandestine military manoevres in anticipation of opposition created rumours of the imminent arrest of the conspirators. Carson left London abruptly and withdrew to the fastness of Craigavon, now turned into an armed headquarters. This scare led to partial mobilisation of the UVF who protected their arms dumps and the homes of prominent UVF leaders. Apparently messages alerting UVF, members were flashed across cinema screens in Belfast.[23] This alert lasted for almost a fortnight and was finally ended with the Curragh Mutiny. It now meant, that through its own lack of resolve, the Liberal administration was now paralysed, and it had simultaneously weakened the position of the only strong constitutional party in Ireland.

Arguments between the Liberals and Conservatives continued throughout the Summer about the terms of the Home Rule Bill, its opt-outs the geography of exclusion which appeared to the bored Churchill as more sessions about 'the dreary spires of Fermanagh.' Derry City was in and out of opt-outs, but generally in, along with Newry, as measures to appease Redmond.[24] The ungainly revolutions of this constitutional carousel were to be dramatically interrupted with the assassination of Archduke Ferdinand at Sarajevo, 28 June. This caused the further postponement of the Home Rule Bill. It was passed on 18 September, and simultaneously suspended until after the war.

During this period of government paralysis it became clear to Eoin McNeill that Nationalists had an opportunity. He proposed to Joe Devlin in the UIL office in Dublin that the parliamentary leaders, validly elected in Ireland, should declare themselves as the proper authorities for administering Ireland. They should set up a committee for that purpose in rooms in the Mansion House and with the British Government having pledged to give Home Rule, declaring war on behalf of small nations, they could not resist a proposal of this kind. Devlin's reply that it was too big a responsibility disheartened McNeill, and convinced him that the future of the UIL was doomed.[25] It is remarkable how prophetic MacNeill's proposals were; four years later they were implemented by Sinn Féin.

Bishop McHugh, meanwhile, in response to the rampant self-confidence of Derry Nationalists tried to win back some ground in June. Rumours abounded, not suprisingly in the constitutional stalemate, that Derry City was to be permanently excluded, along with the six counties. This aroused belligerent speeches from the Volunteers and Bishop McHugh saw a chance to intervene and retrieve lost ground. He arranged a mass rally of all Nationalists which passed pious resolutions of loyalty to Redmond and opposition to exclusion. He also attempted to set up a quasi-political diocesan structure on the basis of these resolutions. This failed miserably as the well meaning resolutions had no alternative means of support in the event of rejection. He was to some degree at the wrong end of Stalin's rhetorical question, "How many divisions has the Pope?". He further compounded his error by forming an independent party at Omagh to pressurize Redmond, at that time attending the Buckingham Palace Conference with the Liberals and Unionists.[26] This too was to no avail, and left Bishop McHugh disillusioned but Mr Redmond and the war were to rescue him from his parochial dilemmas.

Initially Redmond, in his speech of 3 August 1914, pledged Ireland's support for the war, and asked the government to leave the defence of Ireland to the Irish Volunteers and Ulster Volunteers.[27] This caused unease among the IRB section of Irish Volunteer leadership, but Eoin MacNeill's call for calm prevailed. Redmond was about to bring matters to a head, in a way that still puzzles commentators. Two days after the suspended Home Rule Bill had been given Royal assent, Mr Redmond on his way home from Westminster, on 18 September, paused on his journey to address a parade of Irish Volunteers in Woodenbridge. In what can only be seen as a spontaneous speech he urged the paraded Volunteers to regard themselves 'as men, not only in Ireland itself, but wherever the firing line extends, in defence of right of freedom, and of religion.'[28] This was in contradiction of his speech of 3 August and was virtually offering the Irish Volunteers to the British Army.

The effect of this not unexpectedly was divisive within the higher echelons of the Volunteers. The IRB led group split, with a small minority following (approximately 22,000), while Redmond appeared to have retained the vast majority of around 156,000.[29] From then on the Redmondites were known as National Volunteers, while the minority adopted the name of Irish Volunteers. Though small this latter group was led by a determined resolute and highly motivated core, comprising the future leaders of the Rising. Thus the effect of the war and Redmond's miscalculation helped to create a militant, armed group whose aim was insurrection and revolution. Commentators charitably have ascribed Redmond's Woodenbridge speech to a grateful response for the passing of the Home Rule Bill. It should also be seen in the light of the all pervasive jingoism which characterised that period, and remembered that the fraught Redmond spent much of his time amid this atmosphere in England.

Meanwhile in Derry the Irish Volunteers survived the departure in July of Captain "Jack" White, who resigned over differences with the county Board of the Derry and Inishowen Battalion. It was understood by *The Derry Journal* that he had reduced an officer for alleged insubordination, who had later been reinstated by the Board. Captain White asserted in an interview with *The Derry Journal* that he was as eager as ever to place his services at the disposal of the Irish Volunteers.[30] So there passed at this point from the Derry stage a strangely colorful character, who was to reappear, ironically on the eve of another war attending the political salon of the socialists, Tom and Agnes Finnegan, at Magee College in the late nineteen-thirties.[31] As the leadership split, so also did the local battalions, with the Irish Volunteers comprising around 150 members with 17 rifles and the National Volunteers having over 4,000 with 260 rifles. The UVF, were estimated to have over 4,000 rifles in Derry City and County.[32]

On 7 August, the National Volunteers in Derry began to depart in response to general mobilisation. Nearly a thousand men left Derry by train to join the Royal Inniskillings, the Dublin Fusiliers and the Connaught Rangers. The local UVF were to become part of the ill-fated 36th (Ulster) Division who were so appallingly slaughtered at the Somme in July 1916. It is noteworthy that while the military authorities trusted the UVF to form a single division of their own, they would not accord that privilege to the National Volunteers. One can only speculate that this arose from suspicion that to arm and train a numerous, politically motivated, anti-English group would be bordering on the reckless. On the other hand it may have been their assessment of the National Volunteers' discipline, viz that it would involve a prolonged period to develop them into a fighting unit. Certainly General McCready, during the Home Rule crisis of late May 1914, believed that in the case of conflict between the UVF, and the IV, that the latter would indulge 'in an orgy of riot and murder.'[33] At its most superficial this could be myopic military establishment thinking, with racist undertones, but, ironically, it was to be an accurate description of the Tans and UVF in post war Ireland. Even at the rail stations when the first Derry recruits were departing for their regiments, an abrasive partisan atmosphere developed among recruits and followers, as though the Great War as it was to be called was only a sideshow to the timeless epic struggle between two traditions in the ancient city.[34] There is no question that most of the National Volunteers believed they were fighting for the integrity of small nations, particularly Ireland.[35] They accepted that the suspended Home Rule Bill would be enacted at the end of a war, which all and sundry had convinced themselves would be over by Christmas.

By the end of 1914 the scene in Derry had undergone dramatic changes. The initial rise of the Irish Volunteers had given new confidence and independence to Derry Nationalists, while the UVF looked on demoralised. Bishop McHugh had made futile attempts to regain political influence, but events on the national and world stage were to save him from his political Purdah. The lack of determination of the Liberals created another Home Rule crisis, and heralded the first realistic intimations of Partition. In Derry, uneasy Nationalists, their defence forces split, began to drift away to war or in larger numbers, towards a nervous neutrality, awaiting the much heralded end of the war. The arming of the Nationalists, in reaction to the UVF, the Liberal vacillations on Home Rule and the advent of war were to contrive at a situation where the IRB, in a resolute and calculating revolutionary conspiracy, took control of the small breakaway group of Irish Volunteers and planned to exploit Ireland's opportunity from England's difficulty.

CHAPTER THREE

1916-17 CHALLENGE TO CONSTITUTIONALISM

In retrospect, Redmond's policy of involving the National Volunteers in the war was to be viewed as a mistake, though this only became clear much later, around 1916. The immediate beneficiaries of this policy were the IRB. The UIL was to retain, for at least another eighteen months, the virtually unchallenged leadership of the majority of Nationalists. This manifested itself in various ways. The ambivalent indecisive Liberals were caught in the futility of an evenly divided cabinet, those supporting coercion, and those in favour of voluntarism which only retarded decision making.[1] This period, during 1915, was not surprisingly dominated by the war. It had a considerable effect on Nationalist politics, with Redmond accepting and being ensnared in the nether world of postponement of Home Rule which limited his political effectiveness. The Unionists initially benefited with the formation of a coalition government in May 1915 on the demise of the last Liberal Government ever. The Ulster Unionists now had strong supporters in the government, including their inspirational leader, Edward Carson, who reportedly accepted the post of Attorney-General with reluctance; the treasonous poacher had become judicial gamekeeper. Meanwhile the IRB, was covertly infiltrating and controlling the Irish Volunteers and moving towards concrete plans for the Rising.[2]

The apparent strength and standing of the UIL in general, and Redmond and Devlin in particular, can be assessed in how they were received as they conducted their "war policy". Early in the year, 18 January, Joe Devlin inspected the Irish Brigade (Royal Irish Regiment & Connaught Rangers) at Fermoy.[4] The regiments numbered among their recruits many Derry and Belfast men, including Captain McManus, formerly commander of the 2nd Derry Regiment, National Volunteers. Mr Devlin reminded them that the Irish Brigade of 1915, 'were fighting not only for the security and safety of these islands but for the sense of Nationality and Liberty the world over.'[5] This was an obvious coded reference not only to "plucky little Belgium" but to Home Rule for Ireland after the war, which was now the entire basis on which the UIL appeal rested.

This theme was continued more overtly by John Redmond who, spending a few days in Manchester in preparation for St Patrick's Day, addressed meetings in the Free Trade Hall and the Grand Theatre. Mr Redmond commended the great number of Irishmen in uniform, and hoped the 'co-mingling of English and Irish blood on the battlefield,' would help heal the divisions and hatreds after the war,[6] and that the new Constitution (Home Rule) they had won might be inaugurated in a country "purified by sacrifice among a people united by the memory of a common suffering".[7] Of the 100,000 Irishmen recruited by 15 February 1915, 20,000 had been Irish Volunteers, and 23,000 Ulster Volunteers. Redmond estimated, including Britain and the Colonies, that there were at least a quarter of a million Irishmen in the war so far. Redmond finished by saying that 'in fighting for the Empire we are fighting for Ireland. Every Irish soldier who gives his life on the battlefield of Flanders dies for Ireland, and her liberty as truly as any of heroes and martyrs of the past.'[8]

It is worth noting some of the detail of these speeches with a view to exploring two factors. Firstly, Redmond's speech in particular, reflects the jingoism of the age; the call to arms, the unselfconscious acceptance of death as almost a welcome price to pay. What is heard in Redmond's words is probably only a reflection of the almost hysterical, Nationalistic flag-waving imperialism which was commonplace in Britain. However with the accelerating rise of casualties from Aisne to the slaughter of the Somme and Paschendale in 1916, this type of jingoism was to die forever in the blood-sodden trenches of Flanders, with only faint reverberations of it to be heard in siege-conscious Protestant Ulster. Secondly it is disquieting to note the similarity at times of Redmond's rhetoric with that of Pearse in their attitude to the much examined theory of blood sacrifice. Redmond was asking men to sacrifice themselves ostensibly for the principle of liberty and Nationalism, though informally, as guarantors of Irish Home Rule, while Pearse directed the sacrifice to Irish nationhood in its ancient cultural anti-colonial fight. While Pearse called upon the example of Cuchulainn, the mythic hero of Ulster, the Hercules of Irish Nationalism, who lived a short heroic life so that posterity would revere him, Redmond spoke of defence of Empire and Liberty and the integrity of small nations. It is arguable that both are united in rhetoric, with Pearse seeing blood-sacrifice bringing Redemption (a Free Ireland) through martyrdom, and Redmond speaking of "co-mingling blood" and "martyrs of old", their differences are in degree rather than in kind, and both indeed may have reflected the ambience of war more than was thought, though Pearse had been building a Nationalist ideology around Cuchulainn since his college, St Enda's had been founded.

One thing seemingly unaffected by the war in January 1915, was the Derry Corporation's annual election for mayor, which was to remind its citizens of the injustice of the Corporation's political composition. *The Derry Journal* was to fulminate for two columns on the injustice of the gerrymandered Unionist majority and their unwillingness to compromise with the under-represented Nationalists. It recounted the speech of Councillor Hugh C O'Doherty[9] questioning the validity and morality of their stance maintaining:

> ...that the rusty bars of prejudice erected by a clique to prevent a Catholic nominee ever reaching the mayoral chair should be relegated to their proper place on the scrap heap.

The *Journal* concluded that the majority of Derry Corporation, representing a citizen minority, conspired for their own ends under the banner of "Civil and Religious Liberty".[4] What obviously made the municipal charade more objectionable for the local Nationalist population were the reported remarks of the outgoing Mayor, Sir William McLearn. He was attacked by the Nationalist Alderman Logue for insulting the Catholic/Nationalists by suggesting in a press interview that only those 'in the North are industrious and successful. The rest of Ireland is slothful, unprogressive and under the heavy hand of the priesthood.'[10]

It was not unexpected that Derry would be affected by the war in general and the rhetoric in particular. On Redmond's earlier re-assurances that Derry would have the option to secede from the excluded area, the hierarchy broadly supported the war effort. It also helped that Belgium was mainly Catholic, and that Cardinal Mercier's ill-treatment by the Germans had been afforded great publicity in Ireland.[11] The Bishop and Clergy had regained some lost ground in terms of political control since the war, with Home Rule being on the Statute Book, and crucially, because of the split in the Irish Volunteers. They now felt secure enough to virtually re-impose their ban on Irish Volunteer or IRB, activists. This went so far as Clonmany clergy forcing an Irish Volunteer Unit to disband at Desertegney in County Donegal.[12] Bishop O'Donnell of Raphoe was more circumspect in his attitude to the war and didn't quite support Redmond's Faustian deal of recruits for Home Rule. This was not because of any ethical fastidiousness, but because he did not trust the British.[13] In Derry City recruiting was good but in the County areas of Derry and Donegal farmers' sons ignored all calls to join the army.[12]

The National Volunteers were still active early in 1915 in Derry, amid all the war rhetoric, though they were diminished in interest and in numbers. On 16 March they had a route march with band from the Shamrock Hall led by Captain Joseph Campbell. Battalion Commander Healy took charge of rifle drill, and was quoted in the Derry Journal as saying that though their numbers were small, they would improve. On 18 March they held a meeting to discuss the forthcoming convention and review to take place in Dublin on Easter Sunday. The Derry & Inishowen battalions were congratulated on a great display in Celtic Park under the inspection of Colonel Moore, held earlier in the year. Mr E T Duffy speculated that Derry City and District should be able to send several thousand men to the Dublin Review.[14]

The RIC reported that on 11 March only 20 Volunteers (18 armed), took part in the Derry route march with the band, which implied there may have been more bandsmen than Volunteers, and on 18 March, 14 armed Volunteers participated in the route march. Close to the time of the planned review in Dublin, 53 armed National Volunteers drilled in Celtic Park. This was a far cry from the heady days of late spring 1914, when Derry City alone had 5 battalions of Irish Volunteers, one of which numbered one thousand men. There had been no drilling or marching during January and February 1915 and not much party-political activity except at council level, as reported, which on the Nationalist side was mainly re-active, rather than pro-active. Police intelligence ascribed the diminished political activity on the part of UIL to the realization by Nationalists that with Home Rule on the Statute Book, little remained to be done. The Inspector General also reported that 'the people of Ireland are everywhere loyal to the Empire in the war except for Sinn Féin and other extremists.' He was obviously interpreting a veiled and possibly uneasy neutrality in a way that would please his masters. It was clear that Redmond and Devlin were openly pursuing their recruitment policies, obtaining credit for recruitment that would have occurred anyway, to strengthen their hand against a coalition government under Carson and Balfour. The apparent stability of the UIL in Ireland was therefore qualified by certain realities, the fear of conscription, and the complete aloofness in rural areas, particularly of farmer's sons, from the recruitment campaign.[15] They could not, on any count, be prevailed upon to join, and they were to prove willing recruits to any virulent anti-conscription campaign. Fr McCafferty Adm, Letterkenny, stated that sending National Volunteers (Irish Brigade) to France and Belgium was to play into the hands of the Unionists. This struck a chord in the minds of many Northern Nationalists.

Superficially, it appeared at this stage that Redmond's policy was working, he still maintained the confidence of rank and file Nationalists, with clergy at best supportive and at worst neutral. The IV and IRB were apparently sidelined, and opinion among British Tories was beginning to warm to him and the Irish support of the Empire in its hour of need. Evidence of the latter was reported by London correspondent of *The Independent* who recounted on the anniversary of the Curragh Mutiny, 20 March, that opinion in the capital was changing from one of antagonism to one of gratitude and admiration for the performance of Irish soldiers at the front.[16] The correspondent cast doubts on the future of Carsonism after the war. Possibly because of this wave of support for Redmond, a particularly nasty piece of Ulster Unionist propaganda was disclosed by Mr S L Hughes MP, Liberal member for Stockport who, writing in *Reynold's News*, recorded his approval of the Irish soldiers who rescued a group of Gordon Highlanders from overwhelming numbers of Germans. The Scottish soldiers were greatly relieved, to hear the approaching voices of the Connaught Rangers singing "God Save Ireland" after which five hundred of the Irish held off the 2,000 Germans. This story emanated from a private in the Highlanders who revealed the incident in a letter to the press. The MP Mr Hughes while quoting this incident, and referring to O'Leary the famous recipient of the Victoria Cross from Cork, was disgusted at coming across a pamphlet containing anti-Redmondite, anti-Nationalist extracts from an Ulster Unionist publication which disparaged the Irish commitment to the war.[17] Mr Hughes energetically attacked this position ,and wondered why he had heard no similar accounts of valour, about the brave "warriors who had defended Captain Craig's headquarters at Craigavon against countless odds and who would surely put the wind up the Kaiser and his legions".[18] *The Derry Journal* also recounted the letter of a prominent Unionist to the *Irish News* regretting the pettiness of his co-religionists attitude to Nationalists in Ireland on St Patrick's Day, while Irish men so bravely defended the Empire abroad. He also defended the actions of Lady Limerick and her friends in declaring a Shamrock Festival in London, which was very well supported, in recognition of the bravery of the Irish soldiers.[19]

The Derry Journal of 22 March recorded a letter of apology from the Orange Order in Limavady to Fr McGlade PP for the behaviour of their members on the previous Saturday and Sunday passing his church.[20] The unusual apology was probably prompted by the neutralizing effect of the war on partisan politics, though it would not have been difficult to imagine the frustration of a congregation, some of whose members were no doubt sacrificing their lives in France and Belgium, being insulted by a group of sectarian bullies who clearly had not envisaged following their example.

It should be borne in mind that *The Derry Journal* fully supported Redmond and the UIL position, to the point where in its 22 January edition it issued a comprehensive supplement detailing the achievements of Redmond and the UIL, from the Land Question, through Education Acts, Old Age Pensions, to the placing of the Home Rule Act on the Statute Book. Its editorial spoke at length of the credit and gratitude due to the UIL and maintained that 'Irish Interests were safe in the hands of the Irish Party (UIL) and its leader, and therefore could say [*The Derry Journal* never at a loss for a histrionic flourish] in the words of Victor Hugo, that the people were marching onwards with faces towards the dawn.'[21]

However elsewhere, events were occurring, articulated in another form of rhetoric contemplating a similar aim, but with altogether different methods of attainment. The Irish Republican Brotherhood, which derived from the old Fenians, was a secret society dedicated to the overturn of British rule by revolutionary means. They had been involved in the founding of the Irish Volunteers, with Bulmer Hobson and the O'Rahilly (not a member) persuading McNeill to help establish that force. They now had placed, within the Volunteers, two thousand of their men, and controlled the executive with their leaders. In July 1915, leaders of the IRB set up a Military Council within the Irish Volunteers with the express purpose of formulating plans for a rising.[22] Towards the end of 1915, this Military Council decided that the insurrection would begin on Easter Sunday, 23 April 1916.[23]

Early in 1916, the Inspector General reported to the Under Secretary for Ireland that the majority of the people were loyal, expecting Home Rule when the war ended, with the only group giving trouble being the Irish Volunteers (sometimes referred to as Sinn Féiners) who were strongly campaigning against recruitment. He reported that the anti-recruitment campaign was gaining new members for Sinn Féin in rural areas, where farmers sons had a marked reluctance to join the army. Sinn Féin had enrolled 830 new members in January alone and were well organized.[24] In the North, Tyrone was seen as the most active county in Sinn Féin and IRB terms. County Inspector Carey reported that recruiting in Derry City was good

but poor in the county. He reported that there was little party politi-
cal activity, or demonstrations. Neither the UVF, or the National
Volunteers, now virtually extinct, had drill or marches according to
Colonel Moore. The Irish Volunteers in Derry were estimated to have
194 members, with 32 rifles, 25 of which had originally belonged to
National Volunteers but were retained when the IV seceded.[25]

When the Rising took place on Monday 24 April 1916, amidst a
great war involving hundreds of thousands of Irishmen, and a com-
plex political situation made more volatile by the suspension of the
Home Rule Bill, it is not surprising that first reactions were puzzle-
ment, as accurate information was not immediately available. In
Derry it was reported, by both Unionist and Nationalist press, that
the population were taking matters calmly and had not reacted one
way or another. As a precaution troops were quartered in the Guildhall and all other troops were confined to barracks. *The Derry
Journal*, in particular, on 28 April reported that Derry inhabitants
had been 'admirably cool and sensible,' and the Unionist Mayor
Alderman R N Anderson, was 'anxious that the city would uphold
its customary reputation for good order.'[26] The editorial of 1 May
congratulated Redmond for his call to the National Volunteers to
help the authorities to restore order, and was attributing blame for
the Dublin lawlessness to the immunity with which Carson and the
Ulster Volunteer Force had been allowed to operate. By the first week
in May *The Derry Journal* referred to the rising as 'a wicked plot to
make the country a cat's-paw of the Germans,' and that it was 'a mad
enterprise'[27] and probably broadly reflected the views of moderate
Nationalists. To illustrate the confusion caused by lack of good com-
munication and military censorship, *The Daily Mail* had described
James Connolly as 'a Belfast Orangeman,' much to the embarrass-
ment and anger of loyal Belfast, whose Orange Grand Master
publicly refuted the story. Some commentators would also say that
such confusion was endemic to all British analyses of Irish affairs.
The Derry Journal also faithfully reported that His Holiness the Pope
had conveyed 'instructions to all Irish Bishops to exhort their clergy
and people to maintain perfect loyalty towards England.' It is noted
that the editorials above appeared in the issues which also reported
the executions of Pearse, McDonagh, and the Dungannon born

Thomas Clarke. As the executions continued, summarily handed down by courts martial, particularly the execution of the wounded Connolly, a spontaneous reaction from Ireland against the harsh vindictiveness began to appear, and the Irish Party (Mr Dillon) moved too late to stay the unthinking military hand which they had earlier supported. *The Derry Journal* published, on 12 May 1916, the reaction of Bernard Shaw, who defended the right of Irishmen to strike for their liberty against a foreign oppressor, England, and informed the British establishment that they had now created martyrs and heroes of the executed leaders, who were now as surely immortalized as Wolf Tone, Emmet and the Manchester Martyrs. The words of the Dublin Protestant in contrast to the editorial of the Nationalist Journal, served to show the layers of complexity that characterizes "the Irish Question".[28] Bishop O'Donnell remained silent though his Administrator condemned the Rising.

In the House of Commons, it was reported that in the aftermath of the insurrection, 14 had been executed, 73 sentenced to penal servitude and 1,706 deported. Among those arrested and eventually deported to Frongoch in Wales were nine Derry men, arrested after martial law had been declared. The following had been taken into custody as well-known Sinn Féiners: John Fox, St Columb's Wells; Patrick Shields, Bogside; Patrick Hegarty, Westland Avenue; Edward McDermott, Westland Avenue; Chas O'Brien, William Street; Joseph O'Doherty, Creggan Street; Vincent O'Doherty, Creggan Street; J O'Duffy, Foyle Street and James Cavanagh, Alexandra Place. A small quantity of rifles and ammunition was found.[28] The police had observed the unfavourable reaction to the executions, and to the peculiar circumstances of the death of the pacifist Sheehy Skeffington. *The Derry Weekly News* had been warned for inveighing against the military policy in suppressing the rebellion, and having been "warned" by the police authorities, apologized.[30] As the memory of the more dramatic events of the rebellion faded, the harshness of the executions without trial, and the unquestionable bravery of the insurgents were to have a corrosive effect permeating the whole of Nationalist Ireland.

All had changed, though not as graphically, or with as much immediacy as Yeats' poetic imagination would have us believe. To give body and direction to the changes, further events, deriving from the political consequences of the Rising and the continuing war had to take place. As a result of the growing anger in Ireland and America, and among Catholic hierarchy to the number and protracted nature of the executions, Asquith felt it was time for a "permanent" solution and Lloyd George accepted the awesome responsibility to provide it.[31] The American reaction was a crucial one, since it could possibly affect the flow of munitions to the hard-pressed Allies, and this was also used by Lloyd George as a means of restraining Southern Unionists. From 22 May to mid-June, Lloyd George negotiated separately with the Nationalists, Redmond, Dillon and Devlin, and the Unionists, Carson and Craig. The virtually air-tight separateness of Lloyd George's negotiating style enabled him to arrange conflicting conditions with each of them which were then packaged into an ambiguous white paper later in the year.[32] Redmond had been promised Home Rule with temporary exclusion of the six counties (including Derry City), while Carson had been promised permanent exclusion. The six counties were 'to be administered by a Secretary of State, with the help of such officers and departments as might be needed.'* Initially Redmond and Devlin believed Lloyd George, but news of the exclusion, whether temporary or not, leaked out from the Belfast Unionist Council on 6 June. Nationalist reaction in Derry was swift and angry, *The Derry Journal* labelling the proposals as 'preposterous,' and adding prophetically that 'homogenous Ulster is not a discoverable entity and there is no possible plan of partition that would not leave the Province a cockpit of intensified political and sectarian antagonisms.'[33] The Nationalists of Derry City, Tyrone and Fermanagh were particularly infuriated that the opt-out clause no longer applied to them. They also feared that a temporary border could congeal into permanent structures. By mid-June the *Belfast News Letter* was intimating that the exclusion was "definite"' being interpreted as permanent.[34] A Council intended to represent the full spectrum of Nationalist Home Rule opinions was called in St Mary's Hall, Belfast on 23 June. Redmond and the leaders of the

* Note that at this stage no form of local parliament, like Stormont, was envisaged. What was on offer was 'Direct Rule' as Unionists referred to the past Stormont era. Stormont ironically was a form of Home Rule for the six counties.

Irish Party were being strongly criticized in Derry for making such an agreement with Lloyd George without prior consultation with their own party followers.

Bishop McHugh disclosed in a letter of 10 June to Labour Alderman McCarron that the Bishops whose jurisdiction covered the six counties were unanimously against the Lloyd George proposals, and endorsed the view of Cardinal Logue that 'it would be infinitely better to remain as we are for fifty years than to accept these proposals.'[35] Six weeks after the Rising these words may sound strange in Nationalist Derry. We have now encountered the dramatic entry of Partition as a realistic option into the political discussions, underlining the fear it engendered in Northern Nationalists, which was and still is largely incomprehensible to Southern Nationalists.[36] The Bishop went on to highlight his greatest anxiety, the vulnerability of Catholic Education, and the practice of religion in an excluded six counties, and finally concluded by bemoaning the fate of Derry City, which secured the parliamentary majority for Home Rule in electing David Hogg, and 'was now to be treated as a castaway.'[37]

After some debate and discussion, Redmond consulted with the Northern Bishops about the composition of the Nationalist Convention in Belfast and a format acceptable to their lordships was agreed. *The Freeman's Journal* published the format as follows:

Members of Parliament	7
Priests (one from each parish)	168
Divisional Executive	
(some of whom priests)	120
County Boards	40
Irish National Foresters	40
Public Bodies	702
Total	1,077

As expected the delegates of Tyrone, Fermanagh and Derry City voted against Lloyd George's proposals and the remaining six counties, manipulated by Devlin and Redmond, and indeed under a threat of resignation by Redmond and Devlin, voted for temporary exclusion. The Derry delegation was led by Fr McFeely PP Waterside, who pungently expressed the anger and disillusionment with the proposals, and consequent loss of trust in the Irish Parliamentary Party. The resolution in favour of exclusion was passed by 475 to 265, a majority of 210. The Derry City delegation voted 30 to 7 against exclusion, with County Derry about even. The result of this conference was to split the Northern Nationalists into three distinct groups. First the pragmatic East Ulster group led by Joe Devlin, who believed that a fair deal could be made after the war. Secondly the border Nationalists, the Derry City, Tyrone and Fermanagh grouping, which fiercely opposed partition though stopping just short of unconstitutional measures. The third grouping, the still muted Sinn Féin, benefited from the slow development of post Rising Anglophobia and the disarray of constitutional Nationalists. Sinn Féin ignored the partition issue altogether in its pursuit of all-Ireland autonomy. This conference was to prove vital in the future disposal of partition as an issue and as a political reality, in how Northern Nationalists would view it, and Southern Nationalists fail to understand it. The consequent dissipation of the strength of Northern Nationalism was to help the progress of Sinn Féin in the following eighteen months. Coincidentally (?) on the day of the Belfast Conference, 23 June, the *Irish Times* published a statement, which categorically declared that Sir Edward Carson had been promised permanent exclusion by Mr Lloyd George.[40] This was given further endorsement by Lord Lansdowne, a landlord with extensive Irish estates, who stated to the Lords on 11 July that any settlement would have to be 'permanent and enduring.' He later admitted that his speech had received prior affirmation from the Prime Minister.[33] On 22 July, Lloyd George told Redmond that the cabinet had decided to treat the settlement as permanent, and thus was completed the betrayal of Redmond, who, unheeding of Machiavelli, had "put too much trust in Princes". Redmond reacted by warning the House of Commons that faith in constitutional methods was shattered, and they could expect national agitation in full sympathy with the Easter Rising.[41]

These events strengthened the alienation of the Border Nationalists, and only increased their anti-partitionism. Tyrone, Fermanagh and Derry City had been promised an opt-out, as areas with Nationalist majorities in the suspended 1914 Home Rule Act, and thus the Lloyd George proposals caused them bitter disappointment. It must be said that acceptance of the opt-out clause carried with it a *sauve qui peut* attitude which would have meant the abandonment of the Catholics in Eastern Ulster. The border Nationalists rationalized their stance by inferring that a four county statelet would not be viable, and would soon be forced to join the rest of Ireland in order to survive. (Interestingly, this view had also been privately held by Carson and Craig as early as 1913.) They envisaged, as an alternative, the coercion of Ulster Protestants into a United Ireland. The view of the Eastern Ulster (mainly Belfast) Catholics, was a pragmatic one; namely, if partition is unavoidable seek the best terms achievable, for which they would need the solidarity of the border Catholics, and this was the nub of the partition question, as seen by Northern Nationalists.

In July 1916, Bishop McHugh was instrumental in setting up an Anti-Partition League in Derry City, drawing delegates from Tyrone, Fermanagh and County Derry. This was augmented a month later by branches in Belfast, Dublin and Limerick and flowered into the Irish Nation League. However, it never became more than a form of extreme constitutional Nationalism, which shared much with the Irish Party it attacked.[43] In any event this breakaway from the Redmondites would create conditions favourable to Sinn Féin. It was significant that in Derry a prominent signatory of the INL manifesto was Hugh C O'Doherty, a solicitor and former Parnellite. The INL was not fated to develop beyond the areas of the border Nationalists, Derry City, Tyrone and Fermanagh. This was early evidence that Nationalist Ireland at large did not share the concern, or display understanding of the now fully emergent question of partition, which was rapidly becoming the main issue in the North.

The two most significant events in 1915 and 1916 were the effect of the continuing war, and the Rising. The first, by not finishing early as expected, had taken Redmond's war policy on a long vulnerable trek, subjected to revulsion at rising casualties, fear of conscription, and the accession to power of a Coalition Government containing his Unionist enemies. The war also offered an opportunity to those who sought to benefit from England's difficulty, and the consequent mishandling of the Rising by Asquith and his government was to accelerate the search for a permanent solution, eventually resulting in a betrayal of Redmond and his party. These events, resulting in the Lloyd George proposals, had an alarming effect on Derry Nationalists, causing alienation from the Irish Party and the formation of an Anti-Partition League. Two very significant dates for Derry and Northern Nationalists in this period were 24 April and 23 June 1916. The Rising and the revolutionary movement it would foster would impact strongly on the whole future of the North. The Belfast Conference on 23 June, was to signal a split in Northern Nationalists about attitudes to partition, reflecting the self-interests of the border Nationalists seeking inclusion in the South in an 'opt-out', arrangement and the pragmatism of East Ulster Nationalists in hostile Unionist territory. While the split among Northern Nationalists was obviously detrimental to their effectiveness in future negotiations, it was also to isolate them politically to a large degree from the upsurge of Sinn Féin in the South. From now on, the issue in the North was partition, who would be in, who would be out, and these were the factors governing the political thoughts of Northern Nationalists to an almost obsessive degree. The excessive nature of this pre-occupation can be ascribed to mainly one thing, fear. They had no illusions about what would happen under a Unionist administration. They had suffered gerrymandering, discrimination, and all forms of insult and abuse to their religion and national identity. The clergy in particular feared the repression of Catholic education and religious practice, and possibly the consequent loss of control due to secularization of education. Unlike their fellow Nationalists in the South who lived among a numerically small minority of Episcopalians, (who were islands of Protestantism in the sea of Catholic Nationalism), the Northern Catholics were confronted by a different type of Protestantism. The Ulster Protestants were mainly evangelical fundamentalists, who had been excluded from the political process themselves until the nineteenth century. Industrialization meant that in the North-East they identified themselves more with Clydeside and Merseyside, than with the rest of Ireland. Whereas Protestants in the South were mainly landowners or big farmers, in the North Protestants were businessmen, tradesmen, small farmers and factory workers. This made it difficult for Southern Nationalists to understand the fears of Nationalists in the North.

Catholics competed at a disadvantage for jobs against Protestants, who themselves had been lured away from effective trade union and labour politics into the Orange Labour Societies. Thus Northern employers divided and conquered. This difference in experience clouded understanding between Nationalists North and South, and so as partition became more and more the issue for Northern Nationalists, so did the incomprehension about the North begin to affect the judgement of Southern Nationalist leaders.

Bishop McHugh in Derry achieved initial success, with the anti-partitionist INL, but it faded through lack of national support, and served only to pave the way for the rise of Sinn Féin in the North. This also reflected the fear of Nationalists of a split in face of Unionist hostility. The IRB leaders were using the opportunity offered by being political prisoners to organize. This was a field in which a young Cork man, Michael Collins, was achieving prominence.

CHAPTER FOUR

TOWARDS PARTITION

Few would dispute the proposition that the years 1918-21 were one of the most momentous periods in Irish history. This period included the installation of the first Dail, the Anglo-Irish Treaty, the eventual political supremacy of Sinn Féin throughout Nationalist Ireland, and above all the partition of the country into two states. This was followed by a civil war in the southern state, which was instrumental in shaping the format of its political parties to the present day, and whose impact on the north for both Nationalists and Unionists was mainly negative. Critically the civil war gave the Unionists in the north and the British Government a freer hand in setting in place the structures of Northern Ireland, ie police, education and local government with, the minimum of interference from southern politicians or the IRA. By then events had moved to a stage where northern Nationalists were losing any power to influence affairs, whereas, formerly, Derry City had been a pivotal constituency in Ulster terms, and Joe Devlin of west Belfast had been one of the most effective leaders of the Irish Parliamentary Party.

In early 1917, the release of prisoners had brought increased political activity on the part of Sinn Féin. They used their status as the "revolutionaries of 1916", who had fought and died for an independent republic, to very effectively exploit the natural fears of conscription by arguing that without the Rising, conscription would have been implemented. This was a forceful point, and carried great conviction among an apprehensive electorate. Sinn Féin tested their political strength in by-elections, firstly in North Roscommon and South Longford where they won convincingly. It was noted by Inspector General Byrne in his comments to the Under Secretary that 'the conscription policy has captivated the Nationalist youth of the country. Although many of the older converts to Sinn Féin are not Republican it is evident that even they now expect a more ample measure of Home Rule than provided by the existing act.'[1] There were further by-election victories in East Clare (for De Valera) and Kilkenny (Cosgrave) which gave even more momentum to Sinn Féin's growth. In contrast, County Inspector Cary of Derry remarked in July 1917 that Sinn Féin was not making any headway in Derry City, though Sinn Féin flags had been displayed in County Derry.[2] By enforcing Defence of the Realm Act Regulations some Sinn Féin activists and leaders had been imprisoned, notably Thomas Ashe (the commander of successful operations in Ashbourne in Easter Week). Ashe went on hunger-strike as a demand for political status within the prison, and died as a result of forced feeding on 25 September 1917. The IRB and Sinn Féin masterminded his military funeral as a national demonstration of mourning and protest, taking over most of Dublin without interference from the army or police. Significantly, Michael Collins delivered a short panegyric in Irish and English following the volley of shots over the grave side:

Nothing additional remains to be said. That volley which we have just heard is the only speech which it is proper to make over the grave of a dead Fenian.[3]

This illustrates the sharp contrast in style between the pragmatic Collins and the semi-mystical Pearse over O'Leary's grave. The effect of the death of Thomas Ashe and his funeral was to re-invigorate the Irish Volunteers, and confirm the "spirit of 1916".

By August the first Sinn Féin Club had been formed in Derry City, calling itself the P H Pearse Sinn Féin Club, and set up rooms in Richmond Street. While there had been a lack of interest in Sinn Féin in Derry City as already indicated by RIC Intelligence reports, other factors began to influence the Nationalists of Derry. Although Sinn Féin, ignored the realities, viz, northern anxieties about partition, they made political gains from the collapse of Home Rule negotiations in 1916 and later from the eventual failure of Bishop McHugh to achieve any national recognition for his Anti-Partition

League. This discrediting of constitutional Nationalists meant a partial drift to Sinn Féin, at least among the extremists, with only the Ancient Order of Hibernians staying loyal to their president, Joe Devlin. Sinn Féin's anti-conscription stance grew in support among the young and their parents, as news of the slaughter and mounting casualties of the Great War became grimmer. They continued to ascribe the absence of conscription to the Rising and graphically assured the people 'that but for Easter Week their bones would be manuring the fields of Flanders.'[4] Another influence was the succession of Sinn Féin victories in by-elections in the south, especially East Clare for De Valera, which gave rise to the first widespread national displays of public sympathy.[5] While it is true to say that Sinn Féin's following undoubtedly increased in the North, it did not, particularly in Derry City and west Belfast, replace the people's attachment to constitutional Nationalism for reasons that will become clear.

On 2 September 1918, a public Sinn Féin meeting was held in St Columb's Hall addressed by Eoin McNeill and L Ginnell MP. It attracted an audience of 2,500 who, in the opinion of the County Inspector RIC, were there 'mostly from reasons of curiosity.' In confirmation he noted that only ten of the audience returned completed membership applications. More Sinn Féin Clubs were formed in the Swatragh and Magherafelt districts.[6]

In April 1918, the British Government, severely haemorrhaging in man power terms, indicated that the new Military Service Bill would include conscription in Ireland of all men of military age (which they intended to raise to 50). There was a spontaneous outcry from all shades of Nationalist opinion in Ireland, bitterly repudiating England's right to enforce conscription on Ireland. An all-party conference was arranged for 18 April in the Mansion House, Dublin, comprising Sinn Féin, the Irish Parliamentary Party and Irish Labour, to consider the conscription crisis. On the same day a conference was to be held at Maynooth of the Catholic hierarchy under the presidency of Cardinal Logue. The Mansion House conference convened at 10.00am, the Maynooth one at 12.00 noon breaking 2.00pm for lunch, at which time delegates from the Mansion House conference arrived to attend the afternoon session. The

Maynooth conference, with the support of the visiting delegates, issued a clear and very strong directive on the conscription question. They condemned any attempt 'to force conscription on Ireland against the will of the Irish nation' and went on to say:

> ...we consider that conscription forced in this way upon Ireland is an oppressive and inhuman law which the Irish people have the right to resist by all the means sanctioned by the Law of God.[8]

The intensity of the opposition and the solidarity between the constitutional parties and Sinn Féin, allied with the support of the Catholic Church, was enough to forestall any imminent moves on enforcement of the New Military Service Bill. Predictably, reactions to this issue appeared to break down into party lines with Unionist papers supporting conscription, it was felt by opposition parties, mainly to embarrass the Nationalists.

At a packed anti-conscription meeting in St Columb's Hall in Derry, councillor H C O'Doherty pointed out that 'one good thing that emanated from the Irish Convention was that Nationalists and Unionists unanimously passed a resolution advising the government to avoid conscription in Ireland.'[9] It was accepted in Ireland that most rank and file Unionists opposed conscription. A dramatic example was given by a large parade and meeting at Ballycastle arranged by Nationalists and Unionists to protest against conscription. A procession was held before and after the meeting made up of Orangemen, Hibernians and Sinn Féiners who marched alternately to such tunes as "The Boyne Water" and "A Nation Once Again". The meeting was addressed by Louis J Walsh (Sinn Féin) and Mr W J Smyth (described by the Derry Journal rather starkly as "a Protestant"), the latter demanding that their cry be the same as the Belfast shipbuilders who said "We won't have conscription".[10]

However, Derry District Council No. 2, in this sea of unanimity was an island of defiant partisanship. A motion condemning conscription was opposed by Mr T A McElhinney who maintained the 'Nationalists of Ireland had remained at home falling into the good jobs vacated by Ulstermen who went to serve their King and Country.'[11] This was to highlight again what had been a running and bitter dispute throughout the war relating to recruitment figures. As early as March 1915 Redmond had maintained that of the 100,000 recruited to that date, 20,000 had been Irish Volunteers and 23,000 Ulster Volunteers and if Britain and the Colonies had been included there were then 250,000 Irishmen in the war. In August of 1918, the Derry Journal quoted figures given to Mr Joe Devlin (in reply to a written question) which he had received from the Under Secretary of War in April 1918. These figures showed that the total recruitment figure for Ulster was 58,000 of which 20,000 were Nationalist, proportionate to their percentage of the population. Furthermore, in the same answer it was revealed that the rest of Ireland recruited 65,000 of which 10,000 were probably Unionist, therefore according to official government statistic 75,000 Nationalists had joined the army, while the total number of Unionists was 48,000. This, Devlin submitted, once and for all exposed the lies and propaganda emanating from both Ulster and England that Protestant Ulster had given everything and the rest of Ireland, nothing. In proof of Devlin's allegations about propaganda, this section of his speech was reported solely in the Nationalist press.[12]

As the war ended, 11 November 1918, expectations of a settlement to Home Rule and a general election were high. The General Election was indeed called for December. Derry City's Sinn Féin Club had in September already nominated Eoin McNeill as their candidate, much to the resentment of local Nationalists who deplored the precipitate, unilateral action. While Sinn Féin had been clearly victorious in by-elections in the three provinces other than Ulster, the exception being Arthur Griffith's election in Cavan, and had made substantial political gains from their anti-conscription policy, Ulster had a crucial extra political dimension, partition. An indication of this had been earlier shown in the South Armagh and East Tyrone by-elections, in January and April respectively. These constituencies were in the Archdiocese of Cardinal Logue, who influenced voters against Sinn Féin and its revolutionary politics.[13] Partition was a critical issue, which Sinn Féin evaded by throwing the cloak of Republican independence over their own misunderstanding of its complexities. In the event, constitutional Nationalists, with good candidates, won both seats and so made Sinn Féin less dismissive of a pact in the eight northern seats, which they would not have contemplated otherwise. These victories appeared to establish that in the north the main issue was partition.

After some local wrangling in northern constituencies, it was clear that there were genuine fears of the northern seats being lost to Unionists due to a lack of unity among the Nationalist parties. This was a reflection of the traditional northern fear of factionalism in the face of strong intransigent Unionism. In Derry there was grave disquiet among Nationalists at Sinn Féin's unilateral and precipitate nomination of Eoin McNeill, though Sinn Féin felt confident enough in their support to ignore the attacks of the now politically discredited Bishop McHugh.[14] The leadership of Sinn Féin tended to be lower middle class, shopkeepers, publicans, clerks, with a sprinkling of professionals, teachers and lawyers. They particularly drew support from the young and even active sympathy from younger Catholic curates in Derry and Donegal.[15] As a result of pressure from Cardinal Logue and northern bishops, Dillon and De Valera, later replaced by Eoin McNeill, met to arrange a pact for the eight northern seats. Eventually, Dillon and McNeill agreed on 3 December to an equal division of the eight marginal seats and left the potentially contentious allocation of specific consitituencies to Cardinal Logue.[16] Derry City was assigned to Sinn Féin, where McNeill had already been nominated.

A public meeting of Derry Nationalists was held in St Columb's Hall on 11 December 1918 to demonstrate their unity and support for the pact candidate Professor John McNeill. Professor McNeill, in a wide ranging speech attacking the British government and the inconsistencies of the Unionists who condemned Irish Independence as dangerous to prosperity, began his speech by addressing the topic of proposed secularization of education by Sir Edward Carson and all that it implied for the North.[17] In making the education issue an important one he may well have been responding to the fears of northern Catholics as enunciated by Bishop McHugh in a letter to *The Derry Journal* on Friday 6 December. His lordship greatly feared losing the clerical stewardship of the schools, which his laity had built and paid for and moreover was alarmed at handing them over to those who were 'overtly hostile to every Catholic sentiment.' He continued by expressing concern about divorce being available in the six counties, and bequests for masses no longer being legal as charitable offerings; he also donated £10 towards Professor McNeill's election expenses.[18]

Councillor H C O'Doherty also spoke at the St Columb's Hall meeting and pointedly referred to the important role played by Irishwomen who had suffered great emotional loss in the emigration of the young for generations.[19] H C O'Dohertry was the only speaker that night to show any political awareness of the fact that the newly passed Representation of the People's Act had meant a revised poll, enfranchising women for the first time. This was particularly significant for Derry, which had drawn many women of all ages from Donegal and County Derry into its shirt factories for the previous forty years, resulting in a gender imbalance which had militated against Nationalists in previous elections. Indeed it was largely due to the traditional generosity of these women that the Derry churches and schools, over which Bishop McHugh agonised, had been built. McNeill's success was to a large degree attributable to this revised poll (Derry's electoral roll had gone from 6,000 to 16,000). Rev L Hegarty, who chaired the victory meeting for the new Derry MP, referred to this when he specifically congratulated the women of Derry for their contribution to McNeill's election.[20]

Sinn Féin had swept the country, making the Irish Parliamentary Party an irrelevance (in which direction they had been moving since September 1914). They took 73 seats with their president in Lincoln Gaol and 33 imprisoned elsewhere, while the Irish Party only held West Belfast and Waterford, apart from the four Ulster pact seats. Joe Devlin, held in great affection by his own constituency, had easily defeated De Valera in West Belfast, by 8,488 to 3,245. John Dillon, the Irish Party leader, had been heavily defeated. However this was not a nationwide conversion to revolutionary politics, but rather in the main a collapse of confidence in the Irish Party's ability to deal with the Liberal Government and two consecutive coalitions.[21] Disillusioned Nationalists were now seeking a more determined leadership that would get them better terms. Most constitutional Nationalists could not have remained unaffected by the Easter Rising and its aftermath, and the anti-conscription issue

63

Women from Donegal and County Derry made up the bulk of the work force in the city's shirt factories.

had carried them even further from their relatively moderate positions. In Derry the failure of Bishop McHugh to gain national support for his Anti-Partition League had added to local Nationalists' disillusionment.

When the new Dail convened in the Mansion House on 21 January 1919, the 27 Sinn Féin Representatives still "at large" listened to a reading of the "Provisional Constitution of the Dail" followed by "Ireland's Declaration of Independence" and the "Democratic Programme of Dail Eireann" which was unanimously adopted. These institutions and programmes were regarded as theoretical by Collins and his IRB activists who considered their priority as expelling the English first and dealing with administrative matters second.[22] Partition as an issue and strategies for addressing it were barely mentioned. It is worth calling attention to part of the speech of Richard Mulcahy which has layers of future irony for later generations of northern Nationalists:

A nation cannot be free in which even a small section of its people have not freedom. A nation cannot be said to live in spirit or materially while there is denied to any section of its people a share of its wealth and the riches that God bestowed around them.[23]

The main plank of Sinn Féin policy at this time was to seek recognition for Dail Eireann at the Peace Conference in Paris.

Throughout 1919, the post war slump caused labour turmoil in Britain and Ireland. As most union activists in the south were Sinn Féin, this created tensions in the movement, particularly among farmers who did not welcome incessant wage and conditions demands from their labourers.[24] The General Strike spilled over into Belfast and involved workers who were united in non sectarian solidarity. In Derry however a branch of the Ulster Labour Association had been formed in advance of a mass meeting of workers at the Guildhall in February. It had been founded by Sir Robert Anderson, shirt manufacturer and defeated Unionist candidate, which reflects the extent of its radicalism. The obvious purpose, of course, of this association was to reassure Protestant workers of job security and future job patronage on condition they did not join with fellow

Catholic workers in radical organisations such as Trade Unions. The ruthlessness of Protestant employers in dealing with Protestant union activists had a salutary effect on the workforce, already subject to the pressures of high unemployment. The timing of Sir Robert's setting up of his Unionist Labour Association was designed to undermine the mass rally at the Guildhall on 19 February. While there was a lot of militant rhetoric at this meeting it was decided that a ballot would need to be taken on direct action, which in effect was a postponement and thereby disheartened the radical activists.[25] The Union situation in Derry had not been helped by the actions of Peadar O'Donnell, IRA man and ITGWU organiser, who himself admitted in 1983:

> the ITGWU entry into Derry was a mistake and ultimately divisive. Unionisation in Derry was already adequate and the ITGWU's identification with Irish Nationalism in Derry coincided with the outbreak of hostilities between the IRA and Britain, and only served to heighten divisions between workers of different political and religious persuasions.[26]

The Carter's Strike of March 1919 which was bitter and non-sectarian was defeated when it succumbed to the endemic pressures of sectarian vested interests.[27] Added to the labour unrest had been the commencement of the Anglo-Irish war, which is considered to have begun with the shooting of two RIC men at Soloheadbeg in Tipperary on the same day the new Dail convened. With the eventual failure of the Dail delegates to attract any support at the Versailles Conference, it now appeared to Sinn Féin that Irish Independence would have to be won in Ireland, not in Paris or Westminster.[28] From April the IRA military campaign intensified.

In Derry the Unionists Party continued to administer the city from a gerrymandered council while the P H Pearse Sinn Féin Club pledged its support to the Sinn Féin candidate in the North Derry election, which resulted in an increased vote for the Republican Patrick McGilligan. This was evidence that northern Nationalists still hoped Sinn Féin would be an effective defender against inclusion in the six counties.[29] The military campaign of the IRA south and west combined with the tension in awaiting some form of settlement was creating dangerous undercurrents. The apparent inability of Dublin Castle to deal with the situation was producing in all Nationalists an expectation that independence was inevitable. This sense of Nationalist unrest expressed itself in Derry on 15 August when the traditional Nationalists parade demanded the right to walk on Derry's Walls. This resulted in a serious sectarian riot, necessitating army intervention to help the police.[30] This particular incident serves to show the extent to which religion and politics had become inextricably linked in Ireland, since the relationship between the Assumption of the Blessed Virgin and Derry Walls can only be at best, tenuous.

On 12 September Patrick Shiels, a Derry IRA leader and Sinn Féin activist, was arrested for allegedly threatening the police with loaded revolvers during a house search. The P H Pearse Sinn Féin Club had left its Richmond Street, premises under threat of eviction in October, and by December had been refused temporary accommodation for their meetings by the AOH and the United Irish League.[31] This revealed how brittle and ambivalent was the liaison between Sinn Féin and Derry Nationalists where other issues were more relevant than in the south. There was also some degree of tension and unease within the Sinn Féin Executive itself which was recounted in RIC Intelligence reports which stated:

> A reliable informant states that a split has occurred in the Sinn Féin Executive. He states that at a meeting in Dublin on the eve of the suppressed Ard Fheis, Messrs. John McNeill and James O'Meara MP's, deprecated the murders and outrages committed throughout the country which they alleged the public attributed to Sinn Féin. Some of those present protested against the introduction of such matters and a stormy scene ensued.[32]

Sinn Féin and the Nationalists, at the end of September were concentrating their energies on revising the political register for the 1920 Municipal Elections. There is no doubt that the bulk of this work was done by Nationalists, who had built a formidable lore of local electoral information aided by the very effective veteran election agent Michael Mcdaid.

Meanwhile, throughout 1919, the British Government had been working on how to replace the ill-fated 1914 Home Rule Act, then still in suspension. By November most Nationalist politicians anticipated that some form of partition would be advocated. In the event, Lloyd George's provisions in the Government of Ireland Bill 22 December 1919 allowed for two parliaments, one in six-county "Ulster" and one in the 26-county South. It also proposed a Council of Ireland composed of twenty representatives of each parliament, which could eventually, without reference to Westminster, be converted into an all-Ireland Parliament.

Sir James Craig had dissuaded the Committee on the Situation in Ireland from setting up a nine-county state but settled for the six-county option as containing a more manageable Catholic minority. The Catholic minority in nine-county Ulster was 43.7% but in the six counties was only 34%.[33] (Significantly the 43.7% deemed as "unmanageable" by Craig was almost exactly the Catholic percentage of the six county population in the 1991 census.) This Government of Ireland Bill slowly worked its way through a parliament virtually devoid of any Nationalist representation due to the Sinn Féin abstentionist policy, and eventually received the Royal assent on 23 December 1920 to become the Government of Ireland Act. Nationalists still felt that this legislation had an air of unreality and believed it would not be enforced.

In mid January the municipal elections were held under Proportional Representation terms introduced by the British Government in a ploy to minimalise the Sinn Féin vote. It had the opposite effect in the North, where both Sinn Féin and Nationalist coalitions polled very strongly. The municipality of Derry City had been gerrymandered but Nationalists felt that with a well-maintained electoral register they had a good chance of winning. Many demonstrations of Single Transferable Voting were held in local halls to ensure the minimum of confusion. The seasoned Nationalist registration agent, Michael McDaid, and Patrick Shiels of Sinn Féin (until his arrest) had both worked vigorously in the Revision Courts where objections to votes on the register were heard. There was strong motivation among all Derry Nationalists to make a show of strength in response to the introduction of the Government of Ireland Bill on 22 December 1919. This they did achieving a historic victory of 21 seats to 19; the maiden city had finally fallen to Nationalists. Omagh had also been won by Nationalists, and Limavady Council saw Nationalists winning seats for the first time. The effectiveness of both Derry political machines, Nationalist and Unionist, to maximise their respective votes was legendary throughout the British Isles, as was the constituency's renown for close contests. Moreover, in applying their well-honed skills to PR, their efforts were proved supreme in Ireland, when in May 1920, they ranked in the *Journal of the Proportional Representation Society* as having the least percentage of spoiled votes. The North and South Wards both had the highest poll of 93.5%. In Ireland as a whole there was a very low percentage of spoiled votes (2.79% to the apparent surprise of both the British and Irish press), with the North Ward in Derry having the smallest percentage (0.68%) of spoiled votes.[34] The welcome victory for Nationalists was further amplified with the installation of a Catholic mayor on Friday 30 January 1920. The main issues in the election from the Nationalist viewpoint had been asserting Nationalist commitment to a united Ireland, education and housing, as Derry had been experiencing what local papers referred to as a housing 'famine' with many families living in cramped and unhealthy tenement conditions. They therefore saw a victory in Derry as making partition more difficult, or in the last analysis a Derry "opt-out" from the six counties more predictable.

Alderman Hugh C O'Doherty, a local solicitor, former supporter of Parnell and an articulate constitutional Nationalist was the first Catholic mayor of Derry City since Cormac O'Neill, who had been appointed by James II shortly before the Siege and who held office only for a short period.[35] Mayor O'Doherty, in his opening speech, emphasised the historical nature of his accession to the Mayoral chair. He went on to ask the Protestant politicians and citizens of their ancient city to be realistic in this time of change and directly appealed to them:

> Is it not time that you reconsidered your position in relation to your countrymen; that you came to the

H C O'Doherty, the first Catholic Mayor of Derry since Cormac O'Neill during the time of James II. *(Photograph: O'Doherty family)*

conclusion that you owe your allegiance to this land of your birth, and that you should no longer play the part expected of you by English politicians but join with your fellow-countrymen in demanding that the government of this country shall be by Irishmen in the sole interests of Ireland.[36]

Alderman O'Doherty also proposed that the flying of all flags on the Guildhall be prohibited thus ensuring that no citizen be deterred from identifying with his council. He also announced that he would not attend any function where a loyal toast was made or any formal recognition of the British Government was implied. He later had Lord French's name withdrawn from the list of Derry Freemen, on the grounds that he was overtly hostile to the majority of the city's citizens.

Derry Nationalists now felt that they had made substantial gains and were already, to some degree, tasting the fruits of independence. Their victory was a boost to the morale of all Northern Catholics. The Irish News maintained that the loss to the Ascendancy of the maiden city signalled the end of partition as an argument.[37]

Within a few months the feelings of jubilation were to turn to those of alarm as Protestants commenced armed attacks against Catholics. There were serious riots on Saturday 16 April which lasted for hours, culminating in an armed attack by Nationalists on Lecky Road barracks during which at least six civilians suffered gunshot wounds.[38] In a later incident a young Catholic was shot by Protestants at Carlisle Square.[39] The Derry Journal found evidence of careful planning in relation to the attack on Lecky Road barracks. This points to the conclusion that this was the first clear IRA offensive in Derry.[40]

The Derry Journal also traced the origin of the riots to an attack by soldiers of the Dorset Regiment opening fire on a Catholic crowd in Bridge Street consisting mainly of youths, women and children. The following Saturday night two soldiers passing along the top of Bridge Street were attacked by youths in reprisal, leading eventually to a full scale riot.[41] Around the middle of May another more serious riot occurred, when armed Unionists invaded Bridge Street firing revolvers and throwing stones, in retaliation, they maintained

Bishop's Gate, scene of skirmishing and shooting during the June riots, 1920. *(Photograph: Magee College)*

for the shooting of a clergyman in County Down. In the course of the ensuing riot many revolver shots were exchanged from both sides, and after a bayonet charge down Bridge Street, Sergeant Mooney, head of Derry Special Branch, was shot dead on Derry Quay. This again, by the prevalence of weapons in the Bridge Street area, appeared to be an IRA action. Protestant masked and armed gangs from the Fountain Street and Wapping Lane area took over Carlisle Road and commandeered the end of Carlisle Bridge, assaulting and threatening Catholics.[42] Later, a young ex-soldier from Anne Street, Bernard Doherty was shot and killed by Unionists in Orchard Street. The reporting of these earlier incidents serves to show that Derry's June 'riots' or 'war' were not as implied elsewhere the result of an isolated incident in the middle of June but were the culmination of months of armed intimidation by Unionists from the Fountain Street and Wapping Lane area, who appeared, to operate around the area of Carlisle Road/Carlisle Bridge with impunity, under the eyes of an apparently complaisant police force and army. While the leadership of the IRA were later to assert that they did not involve themselves in sectarian conflict, they had certainly on occasion adopted at least a defensive role eg in the Bridge Street area, and an offensive one as recorded already in the attack on Lecky Road police station.

The June episode of rioting, which eventually degenerated into what became known as "Derry's Civil War" began on Sunday 13 June when an excursion party of Nationalists was attacked and fired on by armed Unionists in the Prehen area of the city.[43] The armed men were mainly ex-soldiers from the Fountain Street/Wapping Lane area who frequented the Prehen Wood to indulge in drunken horse-play, no doubt away from the disapproving gaze of their Presbyterian brethren in the Fountain area. There were further attacks on the following Monday and Tuesday nights, with long exchanges of fire between gunmen in the Fountain Street and Bridge Street area, revolver shots being heard from the Nationalist Bridge Street and predominantly rifle fire coming from the Unionist Fountain Street.[44] On Friday 18 June, armed Unionists in the Waterside area of Derry invaded a Catholic district, Union Street and Cross Street, driving out residents, wrecking houses, looting shops and generally creating havoc. *The Derry Journal* of 21 June 1920 recounted the aftermath:

> On Saturday morning these thoroughfares, Union Street and Cross Street presented an appearance as if an avenging army had passed through them, so great was the destruction caused.

The attacks had commenced at 10.00pm and continued until six the next morning, with Unionist reinforcements marching across the bridge during the night. Attempts to rescue the unfortunate residents by boat from the other side of the Foyle were repulsed in an exchange of rapid revolver fire. Residents of the Cross Street area reported that "men in military uniform took part in the attack".[45] The night long devastation and mayhem in Cross Street and Union Street took place only a few hundred yards from Ebrington Barracks, the base of the Dorset Regiment. This raised the atmosphere in the city to a dangerously inflammable level. On Saturday night troops and police took up positions in the usual flashpoint areas, Carlisle Square, Bridge Street, Fountain Street and Wapping Lane hoping to deter an expected riot, or possibly to defend the Protestant areas from reprisals. However, the riot developed that evening in an unexpected area, after a drunken squabble when a revolver was allegedly drawn. This was at eight o'clock at the junction of the Catholic Long Tower Street and the Bishop Street end of Fountain Street. At nine o'clock Unionists poured rifle and revolver fire into Long Tower Street. The first man killed was James McVeigh, a sixty year old resident of Walker's Square whose three sons had served in the army, one having been killed in France. That night five men were shot – four Catholics and one Protestant.[46] Though firing into the Long Tower Street district had commenced at 9.00pm, a strong detachment of the Dorsets did not arrive until 11.00pm, when the Unionists finally withdrew to Fountain Street. The disorder had spread to William Street, a predominantly Catholic area, where some looting of Protestant owned businesses began. At this stage the Irish Volunteers intervened and patrolled the area with hurley sticks.[47]

There was a lull on Sunday, but the following Monday armed Protestants openly patrolled Carlisle Square, controlling access to

Carlisle Bridge and Carlisle Road. That evening, 21 June, they again attacked Bridge Street. On this occasion, as the shooting began to spread to other areas, it prompted the first appearance of a body of Irish Volunteers carrying service rifles, who deployed themselves from Butcher Street firing into Unionist areas. As a result of this apparent threat, an armoured car was quickly dispatched to the Diamond to drive out the Volunteers, but street fighting continued on a widespread scale. Two more Catholics were killed, as well as Howard McKay, the son of the Governor of the Apprentice Boys.[47] Armed patrols now routinely protected the fringes of their respective areas, interrogating, searching and occasionally firing. Sandbagged defences were much in evidence at flashpoints. The reporter of *The Irish Independent* was in no doubt of the scale of the conflict saying:

...the term 'rioting' does not give an adequate idea of the situation. It was war pure and simple. For the last few days Orangemen have more or less dominated the situation, but it was indicated on Monday that their domination was no longer maintained.[48]

The same Monday night attacks had been made on the Bishop Street area by Protestant gunmen from Abercorn Road and Barrack Street, with fire concentrated on St Columb's College. When the President of the College asked for assistance in defence of the College, after it was again attacked the following night, the Irish Volunteers assumed responsibility for its protection and the surrounding area.[49] They dislodged Protestant snipers and inflicted substantial casualties, estimated at twenty. At this point the Commandant of the Irish Volunteers issued a proclamation 'that in consequence of the authorities having failed to maintain order they would have to take control of the situation.'[50] They declared that until then they had avoided entering into what was purely a sectarian quarrel but events had reached a stage when they considered it their duty to interfere.[51] With the effective defence of St Columb's and the obvious assertiveness of the Volunteers, resulting in many Protestant casualties, the shooting dwindled, and the British Army intervened on Wednesday afternoon, 23 June. Due to the partisan

Round tower in St Columb's College grounds, the scene of fighting between IRA and UVF in June 1920. *(Photograph: Magee College)*

behaviour of the army in openly fraternising with armed Unionist killers and looters, some RIC officers threatened to resign and complained bitterly to the military authorities.[52]

Eoin McNeill, the Derry TD, had returned to Derry to assess the situation and recorded his reaction in his memoirs:

> When I arrived in Derry... there was a barricade across the public thoroughfare facing Victoria (sic) Bridge, and another of the same kind from side to side across the principal street of the town, William Street. The town was left completely in the hands of the Orange Mob... I went to the Catholic College and lodged there... I saw the windows that had been shattered with bullets. By the time that I came on the scene affairs had taken a turn which I will describe and the British military had come out into the street. In one of those houses a child put its head out of a sky light in the roof and was promptly shot dead by one of the soldiers. This was the only attempt my memory records on the part of the British Government to preserve the King's peace in the city of Derry...
>
> A small body of Irish Volunteers from Derry got together about a dozen of his comrades and threw up a small barricade... they began sharpshooting against the assailants in various buildings. The resistance gave rise to the rumour that Volunteers were marching in a body from Donegal to enter the city.[53]

McNeill's biographer, Tierney, also refers to the claim that "the small body of Volunteers" to which McNeill refers was popularly believed to be an active service unit sent by Collins from Dublin and the memory of their marksmanship was to last for many years. The writer however can find no evidence for this anywhere, but plenty of contrary evidence from local press accounts, and oral accounts of Derry residents at the time, who were indeed able to identify some of the "marksmen", such as Shiels, Fox, Kavanagh, Doherty, McDade and Brady who were also recognised Commanders, and these were joined by several Nationalist veterans of the trenches of the First World War. The latest evidence of this was in the recollections of George Hamill, a well known Derry Union Official in *The Derry Journal* of 19 May 1995.[54]

The IRA had organised the arming and watch duties of the defenders of their areas. Food had been commandeered and supplied to needy families in danger zones, on one occasion a cow being slaughtered in the local abattoir and each family receiving 2lbs of meat. This indicated a good measure of organisation by the IRA and reflected much local support, not surprising considering the nature of the crisis. The one decisive feature to emerge from their confrontation with the UVF was that they were not sufficiently armed to engage in sustained conflict, but should rather rely on superior guerilla tactics and strategy. However the readiness and vigour with which they defended appeared to have ensured that armed Protestant mobs were never to attack Catholic areas in Derry again.

Peace resumed in Derry after that, and several prominent Protestant businessmen publicly thanked the Irish Volunteers for protecting their property, and likewise Captain Wilton was publicly appreciated by Catholics for defending their property from Protestant looters. This lends weight to the theory that the Protestant murder campaign emanated from elements within the Fountain Street area and was not initiated or endorsed by the Derry Unionist leadership. These Fountain Street elements were believed to have been violently reacting to the Catholic assumption of power at Corporation level.[55]

The death toll had been 19 (15 Catholics and 4 Protestants) with countless injured. It was also believed by Nationalists that Protestant dead had been buried secretly during the height of the conflict, though no evidence of this has ever emerged.[56]

An unfortunate sequel to the Derry "riots" ensued in Belfast. Some Protestants fleeing Derry arrived in Belfast, and one of them addressed a meeting at Workman & Clark shipyard inflaming Protestants to attack their Catholic workmates. This was to begin the expulsions of Catholic workers in Belfast. Later that summer and the following year there was wholesale burning, looting and killing by armed Orange mobs, with the involvement of the UVF, and thanks to inflammatory speeches by Edward Carson and misleading news reports in *The Belfast Newsletter*. In total, from July 1920 to August 1922, the Belfast pogroms accounted for the deaths of 453 (257 Catholic), the driving out from their homes of 23,000 Catholics, and expulsion from their workplaces of 11,000 (from a population of 90,000). All Catholic families had been expelled from the towns of Lisburn, Banbridge and Dromore.[57] It was also estimated that 50,000 Catholics fled the North to the South, England and Scotland.[58]

There can be no doubt that Unionists, fearing that the success of the IRA in the South and West might result in a compromise on the six counties, were inflamed by irresponsible politicians and press, and decided to "consolidate" Protestant areas and workplaces, though initially this may have been a defensive reaction. The view of Eoin McNeill was that Protestants were trying to produce a more homogeneous Protestant Ulster.

In the county elections of June 1920, Fermanagh and Tyrone had passed to Nationalist control indeed throughout Ireland, the Unionist controlled only four counties and some of those only with small majorities. As in the 1918 elections it proved the fallacy of the Protestant claim that there was a Protestant homogeneous six counties, as even so-called Protestant areas had substantial Catholic penetration.

With the Truce in July 1921 and consequent talks between De Valera and Lloyd George, the Nationalists in the North became anxious about their position as a result of any discussions. The Government of Ireland Act had come into force in April 1921 and on 7 June the new Northern Ireland Parliament assembled in Belfast City Hall. On 22 June King George V arrived for the State Opening. While Nationalists openly derided the Belfast Parliament, partition was beginning to assume a dangerous air of reality. The Northern Ireland Government looked like it was establishing itself. Lloyd George offered De Valera dominion status for the 26 counties which De Valera refused but offered instead the idea of "External Association". This meant in effect that Ireland was not in the Commonwealth but loosely associated with it by one of De Valera's famously semantic threads.

The anxieties of Northern Nationalists were further compounded by the continuation of the Belfast pogroms, with murder and population displacement continuing apace. An indication of the degree of Nationalist disquiet was demonstrated by the series of delegations during September and October that went to the Dail on behalf of all geographic sections of six-county Nationalists. On 13 September 1921, a delegation on behalf of Derry City Corporation met with President De Valera "to protest at the exclusion of Derry from the rest of Ireland". Present at the meeting were Griffith, Childers and McNeill, the Derry TD. Alderman Bradley, acting as spokesman pointed out that:

> Derry is the second city in Ulster and is by position, population and trade and industry, the capital of North West Ireland. It has the closest relations in business and other intercourse with Donegal from which the British Government proposed to separate it, at the same time separating Donegal from the rest of Ireland, and even from Ulster.

In reply, President De Valera assured them that Dail Eireann would bear in mind the case of Derry City along with other regions of Ulster in any negotiations that might take place.[59] Significantly a month earlier, on 22 August at a private session of the Dail, when pressed by Louis Walsh (Sinn Féin) for a clarification of his Ulster policy, De Valera ruled out force because they lacked the power and 'some of them had not the inclination and moreover the policy would not succeed.' He was vaguely in favour of some form of county opt-out or plebiscite, for example by Tyrone and Fermanagh though Derry City was not mentioned at this stage. It was believed by some, including Lord Midleton, that Sinn Féin were particularly covetous of acquiring Tyrone and Fermanagh, where their party had taken the strongest hold in the six counties.[60]

The Anglo-Irish Conference opened on 11 October 1921 and the Anglo-Irish Treaty was signed at 2.00am on 6 December 1921. News of the Treaty quickly spread to the press and to De Valera's abiding resentment, before he himself had been informed. By 7 December a deputation representing all shades of Northern Nationalist opinion had arrived in Dublin for a Mansion House Conference, seeking elucidation of the Treaty articles with reference to the six counties. Derry City was represented by Mayor H C O'Doherty and Father McFeeley PP Waterside. The Dail Speaker and Eoin McNeill outlined the policy they thought they ought to adopt. It constituted a combination of non-recognition of the Belfast Parliament with a practical programme of "passive resistance". He further asserted that 'the danger in the North is an artificial one although it is a real danger. It has not got the strength of permanency.'[61]

The Mayor of Derry, not noted as a dissembler, came quickly to the point:

> Our representative has given away what we fought for over the last 750 years. It is camouflage. Once the Northern Parliament is put into operation there is a breach in the unity. We are no longer a united nation. You have nothing to give us for sacrifices you call upon the people to make. If in the first instance Belfast contracts out you are handing over manacled the lives and liberties of the Catholics who live in that area. There are no doubt suggestions of guarantees for the minority. What guarantees can be given to minorities in respect of the legislation, in respect of filling appointments. If they contract in, the position you hand to the Northern Parliament is that they have full legislative powers in the Act of Parliament that will enable them to gerrymander us out of existence as they have done from time immemorial. They will be able to fill every appointment. No guarantee is asked from them in respect of any of these matters. We will be ostracised on account of our creed.

Both Dr McNeill and Councillor Shiels (Sinn Féin) from Derry disagreed, again reflecting the tensions within Northern Nationalists due to the partition issue.

Father McFeely pointed out that:

> Belfast would go in for secularising the schools. We could not work under a Belfast Parliament. We abso-

lutely decline to have anything to do with the Belfast mob. We are not able to help ourselves. We want to know if anything can be done for us. This thing is now signed.

Father Mcfeeley's *cri de coeur* held an accurate assessment of the powerlessness of Northern Catholics when faced with a partition solution agreed by their own political representatives.

The next day, 8 December, spokesmen from the deputation met De Valera at 11.00am in the Oak Room at the Mansion House. This was minutes before De Valera was to oppose the Treaty at a critical Cabinet Meeting that morning. To their requests for clarification De Valera replied noncommittally that he could not give them any advice but said the cabinet would be pleased to consider their views. Further pressed on the partition issue he continued:

Until a definite settlement is arrived at, we get on as we are doing; whatever was decided in the past holds good. Until the Northern Parliament is recognised by the Irish people it has no authority in our eyes.

This has the characteristically cryptic note De Valera adopted when he confronted the topic of partition in particular, and the Treaty in general.[62]

The Mayor of Derry's repudiation of the Treaty terms was not reflected in the views of The Derry Journal which saw the Treaty as "An Inspiring Achievement" and like the Nationalists of Tyrone and Fermanagh saw Article 12, referring to the Boundary Commission, as a redemption from the Northern Parliament.[63] Lord Carson, venting his disappointment to the Upper House, maintained that Ulster had been betrayed, and that England had been made 'to scuttle out of Ireland' The signatories of the Treaty had been led to believe that the Boundary Commission would enact frontier changes excluding large Catholic majorities, "according to the wishes of the inhabitants" like Tyrone, South Armagh, and South Down and even Derry City. The effect of this, the signatories believed, would leave the remaining area no longer economically or politically viable, and so it would virtually drop into the lap of the Southern Government. (Significantly neither the Nationalists or Unionists paid attention to the amended version of the original Treaty relating to border changes arising "from the wishes of the inhabitants". The amendment added" so far as may be compatible with economic and geographic conditions".) The optimistic viewpoints on the Boundary Commission appeared to overlook the fact that the Northern Ireland Parliament was already putting into place the administration of education and local government, it had a large and well armed paramilitary police force paid for by the British Government, (Lloyd George later admitted he had armed 48,000 Protestants),[64] and the support of the British Army. It is unlikely that someone as pragmatic as Collins did not have this in mind. In conjunction with McNeill's policy of non-recognition and passive resistance, Collins advocated making the Belfast Parliament unworkable, and while negotiating further with Churchill and Craig had unleashed the Pro-Treaty IRA in the North. This resulted in murderous reprisals in Belfast and the Border areas. Collins' policy was a complete misreading of the Unionists, who, after all, saw themselves as having nowhere to go and thus reacted to attacks with greater determination to hold their existing border. Collins appeared to have contradictory views of the Ulster question. He wrote to Louis T Walsh about the position of Northern Nationalists:

> ...that we stand first in the unity of Ireland, second on the boundaries decided by the wish of the inhabitants. Until one or other is achieved, I have maintained there could be a solid anti-partition party (as one party) in the North East.

The contradiction between the goal of unity and the acceptance of partition implicit in the Treaty made many Nationalists direct their hopes to Article 12 as their only release from an "alien dispensation". They had read about the Treaty debate devoting its most intense rhetorical energies to "the oath" and the nature of dominion status. They read of De Valera's Document 2, its amendments, and its final withdrawal in a haze of unintelligibility (though including an acceptance of the Boundary Commission solution) and remarked that out of 338 pages of debate printed in the Dail Report only nine were devoted to the question of partition, and six of those were contributed by three deputies from County Monaghan.[66] Some Derry and border Nationalists therefore sensed the utter unreality of the approach, or lack of approach of the provisional Dublin Government to the Ulster question. A cover of Republican rhetoric had been flung over its complexities and ambiguities to disguise the Southern incomprehension and/or indifference. Northern Sinn Féin conspired with the Dublin Government to sustain a policy of nebulous national unity that again contradicted the reality of Northern partition. Cahir Healy, a leading Sinn Féin supporter, was to admit in 1925 that 'the Sinn Féin leadership (1918-22) did not understand the Northern situation or Northern mind. Griffith, sanest and best informed of them, nursed a delusion that the beginning and end of the problem lay in London.'[67]

Nationalists in Derry now clung tenaciously to the Boundary Commission as their only hope, defeating a Sinn Féin proposal in January 1922 not to recognise the Belfast Parliament. Bishop McHugh had made a return to politics as Sinn Féin had lost ground in their inability to obstruct partition, and argued that Derry Corporation had to avoid abolition by the Northern Ireland Government, so that a Nationalist corporation would be in place to make a successful plea to the Commission for Derry's inclusion in the Irish Free State. However, a severe shock awaited the Derry Nationalists. In October 1922 the Northern Parliament abolished Proportional Representation, and proposed new municipal elections in January 1923 based on pre-1919 gerrymandered electoral boundaries. This change was designed to strengthen the Unionist case in relation to Article 12 as they could now hope to regain lost councils. In November, at a public meeting in Derry, it was decided to boycott the elections.[68] A Unionist majority was returned in January's election and Derry Corporation reverted to Unionist minority control. Nationalist Councillors were not to return to the council for ten years.

In his final speech as the outgoing Mayor of Derry, H C O'Doherty angrily accused Craig of 'disenfranchising the minority and reducing its members to the condition of serfs.' In refusing Craig's request for Nationalists to attend the Belfast Parliament, Mayor O'Doherty vowed 'So far as I am concerned I will neither dip my beak into his dish nor feed out of his hand.'[69]

Poster urging the boycott of Irish goods. *(Photograph: Magee College)*

The situation for Northern Catholics had been further complicated by the Civil War, but not because the issues which divided
the South weighed heavily with Northern Nationalists. The three
way divergence of Nationalist policies (pact elections aside) had
existed since the Belfast Conference of June 1916, with border Nationalists now exclusively seeking a solution through Article 12, the
Belfast Devlinites seeking recognition of the Belfast Parliament as a
united Nationalist front seeking better terms from it, and finally
Sinn Féin, still adhering to the Dublin "unity first" line. The issue of

Pro-Treaty and "Irregular" did not really arise, except within Sinn Féin and the IRA who in Belfast and Derry were mainly Pro-Treaty. (Frank Aiken of South Armagh was later to defect to the Anti-Treaty side.) The Civil War prevented the Dublin Government, from August on without Collins or Griffith, from giving much attention to the Ulster problem or the mechanics of the Boundary Commission, whose formation was now delayed. The loss of Collins and Griffith was particularly crucial to Northern Nationalists as they were the only members of the Dublin Government who gave any priority to their plight. The Dublin Government's pre-occupation with the Civil War thus afforded the Northern Ireland Government time to consolidate, as it proceeded to do in local government administration policing and education. This was also the period when the divisions and confusion of the Northern Nationalists dissipated their effectiveness and bargaining power in dealing with the Belfast Parliament. An indication of this was in their response to the new municipal elections in January 1923 when Nationalists in Derry City, Dungannon, Enniskillen and Downpatrick boycotted the polls while Armagh, Strabane and Omagh, who maintained their majorities contested, took part, thus presenting an appearance of disunity.[70] It must be borne in mind, however, that Northern Nationalists had been subjected to great uncertainty, and political vacillation from the British Government since the failure of the Home Rule negotiations in 1916.

The last great hope of Derry Nationalists, the Boundary Commission, was already beginning to fade after Unionists resumed control of Derry Corporation in January 1923. Optimism was waning and giving way to thinly veiled desperation. Due to further obstruction by Craig and disarray in a Dublin Government recovering from the Civil War, further delays were encountered in the setting up of the Boundary Commission. This enabled the Northern Ireland Government to further strengthen its administrative and territorial position, to the detriment of Northern Catholics. The Commission finally met on November 1924, the Irish Government representative being Eoin McNeill, one time Derry TD. The Commission made a number of visits to Derry with full hearings on Derry's position taking place in the city from 14 May 1925 to 5 June.

Evidence from both Nationalist and Unionist sides was presented. The claims that the city should become part of the Irish Free State were opposed on the grounds that the greater part of the trade of the city and its port was with Northern Ireland and that the city was linked economically with the Protestant districts of the East.[72] These last points were decisive for Judge Feetham, who invoked the "so far as may be compatible with economic and geographic conditions" clause of Article 12, maintaining that those conditions would take precedence over the "wishes of the inhabitants". This clause was used to the same effect in all parts of Ireland. It was alleged by E M Stephens, Secretary of the Northern Eastern Boundary Bureau, that Derry Nationalists had mismanaged their presentation of their case, mainly because 'they seemed unaccustomed to working together.'[73] Irrespective of the truth of this observation, the fact that all Nationalist areas were included in the six counties against their wishes would make the quality of their submissions appear to have been irrelevant. These findings relating to Derry were leaked to the press, it is believed by Fisher, the British Government representative, on 7 November 1925. In the resultant furore Eoin McNeill resigned from the Commission on 20 November and from the Southern Government a few days later. Eventually after much bargaining and threats, Cosgrave was outmanoeuvred over spurious tax claims and finally on 3 December 1925 signed the Tripartite Agreement amending the 1921 Treaty. This accepted the Northern Ireland border, the six counties, without qualification, and the virtual abolition of the Council of Ireland, for Dublin's release from the concocted tax claims. Cosgrave, to the everlasting bitterness of Northern Nationalists, claimed that he had negotiated 'a damned good bargain.' To the Nationalists of Derry and the border areas, who had supported the Treaty on the grounds that Article 12 would release them into the Free State, now stood abandoned, isolated from the hostile Northern Government and now alienated from what they had once viewed as the friendly Dublin Administration. Furthermore their betrayal and internal exile in their fatherland, was intensified by the lack of guarantee or security of civil rights as expressed by Cahir Healy.[74] The words of H C O'Doherty to the Mansion House Conference on 7 December 1921 now seemed prophetic when he feared that 'they (Dublin Government representatives) were handing over manacled the lives and liberties of the Catholics who live in that area.' Derry's sense of agony and betrayal was heightened and further refined by the experience of having seen from the heights of municipal autonomy, the distant new Jerusalem of National Independence only to fall into the chasms of treachery and intolerance. The populous Nationalist majority was now a sullen and disenchanted minority in its own city now part of that greater disillusioned and demoralised minority of an intolerant, unyielding hostile statelet, Northern Ireland.

CONCLUSION

Certain underlying factors in Ireland, North and South, conspired to advance partition as a solution to the Ulster problem. Firstly, the Protestant majority of the North in numbers and in their fundamentalist nature manifestly differed from their southern counterparts who were patrician, Episcopalian and basically establishment. This made it difficult for southern Sinn Féin leaders to understand the gathering force and intractability of the Northerners' animosity.

Another element was the nature of Irish Nationalism, with its two traditions of the constitutional and the physical force or revolutionary type. The constitutional politicians had been relatively successful in prising concessions from successive British Governments and appeared to be moving gradually towards the attainment of Home Rule. A mistake in earlier Home Rule Bills had been the omission of special treatment for Northern Protestants while they were still unarmed. The undermining of constitutional government by Bonar Law and the Conservatives was largely instrumental in fomenting strife in Ireland. Combined with the Liberal inaction at the formation and arming of the UVF they had paved the way for the replacement of the Irish Parliamentary Party by the Irish Volunteers and Sinn Féin after 1916.

The First World War intervened to provide the IRB with their opportunity from England's difficulty, and to furnish them with the conscription issue which enabled Sinn Féin to sweep the country and eventually to bring to the negotiating table leaders who did not understand the northern mentality.

Florence O'Donoghue maintained that Sinn Féin's political progress, combined with the re-organisation of the Irish Volunteers, was to fuse or synthesize at last the constitutional and physical force traditions of Irish Nationalism.[1] Though this view is debatable it certainly did not apply in the north where the hostile environment did not allow Sinn Féin or the IV to develop deep roots. (There was a dual hostility in some places, from the Catholic hierarchy as well as Unionists.) Also the absence of agrarian agitation and the presence in places like Derry City of clerical dominance for almost a generation made it difficult for the IRA to thrive there. They were also chronically under equipped against much greater odds.

These features finally impacted powerfully on Northern Nationalists, who became the sacrificial victims of intransigence and intolerance on the one hand and misapprehension and evasiveness on the other.

The rise of Nationalism in Derry reflected the changes taking place in the rest of Ireland but also was affected by the changes in Derry itself. Nationalists had a majority in the city since 1851, but due to gerrymandering and limited electoral qualification had minority status at municipal level, and sometimes parliamentary level. The "Land War", which had produced political success and confidence among rural masses in the South and West for the first time in Ireland, was not as relevant in the North East of Ireland, due to the "Ulster Custom" of tenantry. This meant that the masses in the North, except for West Donegal, had not developed the political confidence of their Southern counterparts and so Northern Nationalists were more vulnerable to the stronger clerical influence which had derived from Catholic Emancipation and the "devotional revolution" of Cardinal Cullen. Though this influence was temporarily replaced by the masterly political manipulation of the "Land War" of Parnell, the resentful hierarchy regained lost ground in the divisiveness and disaffection following his decline.

Another factor affecting Northern Catholics was that, in distinguishing them from the Protestant majority, their religion also became the defining factor of national identity. This led to a heightening of religious awareness and sensitivity, and inevitably gave more influence to the Catholic hierarchy. A third element that further contributed to that influence in Derry was the revival of the Columban Tradition, which compounded the intertwining of religious and national identity. From the early 1890s to 1914, the clergy in Derry utilized their influence to deter revolutionary parties and their vehicles, such as the GAA, from recruiting there. They also voiced disapproval of the United Irish League, ostensibly to avoid internecine strife among Nationalists. This resulted in political stagnation at a time immediately prior to the most crucial events in modern Irish history.

The formation of the Irish Volunteers in Derry City in early 1914 was in the main a reaction to the creation of the UVF, and also marked a return to the mainstream of Irish Nationalism. Notwithstanding their enthusiasm and determination, the continued lack of arms was to be a decisive factor in later conflict with the UVF. The split caused by Redmond's committal of the Volunteers to active service in the British army left the residual Irish Volunteers with even less rifles (estimated at 27 by RIC Intelligence Reports), and very ill-prepared for prospective revolutionary action.

The two significant dates in 1916 for all northern Nationalists were 24 April and 23 June. The Rising and its mishandling by the British Army accelerated the search for a solution by the coalition Government and portrayed the IRB and Irish Volunteers as heroes and martyrs in Nationalists eyes. Sinn Féin made political capital out of the "spirit of 1916" and, combined with the conscription issue of 1917/18 (particularly after the introduction of the new Military Service Bill April 1918), swept the country in the 1918 election. They could not have achieved this success without the help of the Coalition Government. The paralysis of the last Liberal administration which had witnessed the flouting of constitutional government by the British Establishment in the arming of the UVF and the Curragh Mutiny, was compounded by the tolerance of treasonous activity in the appointment of Carson to the cabinet. The failure of the Home Rule negotiations in the Summer of 1916, and the humiliation and betrayal of Redmond by Lloyd George, hastened the collapse of the Irish Parliamentary Party, the only serious alternative to extreme Nationalist militancy.

However the swing to Sinn Féin was not entirely a conversion to revolutionary politics. Disillusioned Nationalists turned to Sinn Féin in the hope of securing better terms from the British Government than had been negotiated by the discredited Irish Parliamentary Party. In any case the revolutionary credentials of Sinn Féin with-

out Connolly were always suspect. They certainly had revolutionary method but little ideology. Andrew Gailey's point is well taken,
that concessionary land legislation at the turn of century removed
radical momentum from the Nationalist movement, though new
motivation sprung more from cultural Nationalism.[2] Indeed what
happened in Ireland between 1916 and 1923 could be termed as a
revolution without ideology. Peadar O'Donnell later confirmed this
view when he said 'the Free State was in existence long before the
name was adopted.'[3]

The Belfast Conference of Northern Nationalists on 23 June 1916
proved crucial to the future structure of Nationalist politics. The
acceptance by the conference of partition, albeit temporary, resulted
in a three way split; the border Nationalists, including Derry City,
who sought inclusion in the South by county plebiscite, the East
Ulster Nationalists who pleaded for united Nationalists to make a
deal with Unionism, and Sinn Féin who enigmatically ignored partition in pursuit of Irish Independence. This damaging split endured
right up to the Treaty and beyond undermining their effectiveness
to deal with their abandonment in a hostile administration.

Derry City's position had been further complicated by Nationalists gaining control of the corporation in January 1920. They sensed
that this historic victory foreshadowed, if not complete independence, at least a means of expediting their passage into the Free State
via the Boundary Commission. This Commission, whether intended
to or not, very conveniently fulfilled a role for both parties of nego-
tiators at the Treaty Conference. It became a legislative fig leaf to
cover certain failings on the part of both teams. It enabled Collins
and Griffith to maintain that large tracts of the six counties would
opt-out, leaving an inoperable political and economic residue and
therefore justifying the Treaty. Conveniently it also helped the Dublin Government to evade confronting the well armed northern
Protestants, something for which De Valera had already admitted
in August 1921 they lacked inclination and power.[3] Article 12 also
enabled Lloyd George and Craig to paint a veneer of democracy
over the creation of the six counties in an attempt to appease large
numbers of Nationalists while the Six County Statelet was being
consolidated with British arms and money from September 1920.

The optimism of Derry Nationalists was dealt a further blow when the Belfast Parliament abolished PR in local elections and decreed a return to pre-1919 gerrymandered boundaries. The death of Collins and Griffith in the course of the Civil War virtually sealed the fate of all Northern Nationalists, as they were the only Dublin leaders who gave Ulster any priority. The preoccupation and disarray of the Provisional Free State Government enabled the Northern Ireland Government to consolidate the borders defined in the Government of Ireland Act 1920. Cosgrave, on 3 December 1925, signed the Tripartite Agreement, amending the 1921 Treaty and accepting the six county border in what he referred to as a 'damned good bargain.' Thus Derry's Nationalist majority were now once again a gerrymandered minority in their own city, and were part of the bitter disaffected minority abandoned in an antagonistic statelet.

NOTES

CHAPTER ONE

1. Brian Lacy – *Siege City* (Belfast 1990) p16
2. Brian Lacy – op. cit., p68
3. Brian Lacy – op. cit., p156
4. George Dangerfield – *The Damnable Question* (Boston/Toronto 1976) p71
5. Ibid.
6. Derry Journal – 30 December 1918
7. Peter Alter – Nationalism p4
8. F S Lyons – *Ireland Since the Famine* (London 1983) p130
9. Brian Lacy – op. cit., p186
10. Desmond Murphy – *Derry, Donegal and Modern Ulster 1790-1921* (Culmore – Aileach 1981) p164
11. Desmond Murphy – op. cit., p177
12. Brian Lacy – op. cit., p210
13. Desmond Murphy – P167
14. George Dangerfield – op. cit., p70
15. George Dangerfield – op. cit., p90
16. F S Lyons – op. cit., p114
17. Fr W Doherty – *Derry Columcille* (Derry 1899)
18. Brian Lacy – op. cit., p19
19. Brian Lacy – op. cit., p211
20. Desmond Murphy – op. cit., p171
21. Desmond Murphy – op. cit. p177
22. Sam Hughes – *City on the Foyle* (Belfast 1984) p96

CHAPTER TWO

1. Desmond Murphy – *Derry, Donegal and Modern Ulster 1790-1921* p179

2. Desmond Murphy – op. cit., p178
3. F S Lyons – *Ireland Since the Famine* p300
4. Brian Lacy – *Siege City* p218
5. F S Lyons – op. cit., p304
6. Randolph Churchill – *Churchill* p474
7. George Dangerfield – *The Damnable Question* p61
8. D Murphy – op. cit., p178
9. RIC – Insp. General's Monthly Confidential Reports 1914 CO 904/92
10. Ibid
11. RIC – March Monthly 1914 Report Insp. General CO.904
12. Ibid. – May Monthly Report 1914 CO.904/92
13. Desmond Murphy – op. cit., p180
14. Desmond Murphy – op. cit., p181
15. RIC - Reports – May 1914 CO904/92
16. George Dangerfield – op. cit., p106
17. George Dangerfield – op. cit., p106
18. George Dangerfield – op. cit., 109
19. RIC Reports – County Inspector's Monthly Report – June 1914, CO 904/93
20. Ibid.
21. RIC Reports – May 1914 CO 904/93
22. Derry Journal – 16 March 1914
23. George Dangerfield op. cit., P89
24. Ibid. P128
25. M Tierney – *E McNeill; – Scholar and Man of Action* (Oxford 1980) p147
26. George Dangerfield – op. cit., p182
27. F S Lyons – op. cit., p310
28. George Dangerfield – op. cit., p129
29. Ibid p133
30. Derry Journal – July1914
31. George Hamill – Recollection August 1995
32. RIC Reports – July 1914 CO904/93

33. McCready Annals
34. Londonderry Sentinel – 8 August 1914
35. Derry Journal – 8 August 1914

CHAPTER THREE

1. George Dangerfield – *The Damnable Question* p148
2. Ibid. p155
3. Derry Journal – 20 January 1915
4. Ibid.
5. Derry Journal – 15 March 1915
6. Ibid. – 17 March 1915
7. Ibid.
8. Derry Journal – 22 January 1915
9. Ibid.
10. Derry Journal – 22 January 1915
11. E Blythe – 'Organising the IRB in Donegal' *Donegal Annual 1966* V11 No. 1 p41-42
12. D Murphy – *Derry, Donegal and Modern Ulster 1790-1921* p241/242
13. RIC Reports – April 1915
14. Derry Journal – 22 March 1915
15. RIC Reports – April 1915 CO 904
16. Derry Journal – 19 March 1915
17. Ibid.
18. Ibid.
19. Derry Journal – 22 March 1915
20. Ibid.
21. Derry Journal – 22 January 1915
22. George Dangerfield – op. cit., p136
23. Ibid p155
24. RIC Reports – January 1916 CO 904
25. Ibid.
26. Derry Journal – 28 April 1916

27. Derry Journal – 1 May 1916
28. Derry Journal – 12 May 1916
29. Londonderry Sentinel – 6 May 1916
30. RIC Reports – May 1916 CO 904
31. George Dangerfield – op. cit., p226
32. Ibid.
33. Derry Journal – 7 June 1916
34. Belfast News Letter – 13 June 1916
35. Derry Journal – 14 June 1916
36. Ibid.
37. Ibid.
38. Freeman's Journal – 18 June 1916
39. George Dangerfield – op. cit., p237
40. Ibid. p238
41. Ibid. p239
42. Eamon Phoenix – *Northern Nationalism – Nationalist Politics, Partition and the Catholic Minority in Northern Ireland 1890-1940* (Ulster Historical Foundation, Belfast 1994) p 37
43. Eamon Phoenix – op. cit., p36

CHAPTER FOUR

1. RIC Reports Inspector General July 1917 CO/904
2. RIC Reports County Inspector July 1917 CO/904
3. Tim Pat Coogan – *Michael Collins* (Hutchinson 1990) Page p74
4. RIC Reports Inspectory General August 1917 CO/904
5. D Murphy – *Derry Donegal and Modern Ulster 1790-1921* p243.
6. RIC Reports County Inspector September 1917
7. Derry Journal 8 April 1918
8. Derry Journal 19 April 1918
9. Ibid.
10. Ibid.
11. Ibid.

12. Derry Journal 5 August 1918
13. E Phoenix – *Northern Nationalisim – Nationalist Politics Partition and the Catholic Minority in Northern Ireland 1890-1945* p46
14. Desmond Murphy – op.cit., p251
15. Desmond Murphy – op.cit., p246
16. Eamon Phoenix – op.cit., p51
17. Derry Journal 13 December 1918
18. Derry Journal 6 December 1918
19. Derry Journal 13 December 1918
20. Derry Journal 30 December 1918
21. George Dangerfield – *The Damnable Question* p299
22. George Dangerfield – op.cit., p303
23. Maryan Valiulis – *Portrait of a Revolutionary General Richard Mulcahy and the Founding of the Irish Free State* (Irish Academic Press 1992) p27
24. RIC Reports Inspector General May 1918 CO/904
25. RIC Reports County Inspector February 1919 CO/904
26. P Starrett – *The ITGWU in its Political and Industrial Context* (UU Coleraine 1987) p332
27. Desmond Murphy – op.cit., p19
28. Eamon Phoenix – op.cit., p64
29. Eamon Phoenix – op.cit. p65
30. RIC Reports Inspector General August 1919 CO/904
31. RIC Reports County Inspector October 1919 CO/904
32. RIC Reports Inspector General September 1919 CO/904
33. Michael Farrell – *Northern Ireland, the Orange State* (Pluto Press 1980) p16
34. Derry Journal May 1920
35. Derry Journal 2 February 1920
36. Ibid
37. Irish New 21 January 1920
38. Derry Journal 19 April 1920
39. Derry Journal 21 April 1920

40. Derry Journal 19 April 1920
41. Ibid
42. Derry Journal 17 May 1920
43. Derry Journal 16 June 1920
44. Derry Journal 18 June 1920
45. Derry Journal 21 June 1920
46. Ibid
47. Ibid
48. Derry Journal 23 June 1920
49. Ibid
50. Ibid
51. Derry Journal 25 June 1920
52. Ibid
53. Derry Journal 28 June 1920
54. M Tierney – *Eoin McNeill Scholar and Man of Action 1867-1945* p287
55. Derry Journal 19 May 1995
56. Derry Journal 28 June 1920
57. Ibid
58. Michael Farrell – op.cit., p62
59. Eamon Phoenix – op.cit., p251
60. Derry Journal 14 September 1921
61. John Bowman – *De Valera and the Ulster Question*
    (Clarendon Press Oxford 1980) p61
62. Eamon Phoenix – *The Nationalist Movement in Northern
    Ireland 1914-28* (Ph.D. Q.U.B. 1983) p2
63. PRONI Cahir Healy Papers D2991/B/2
64. Derry Journal 9 December 1921
65. E Phoenix op.cit., p225.
66. F S Lyons – *Ireland Since the Famine* p445
67. Irish Statesman 4 December 1926
    (Letter to Editor from Cahir Healy)
68. Derry Journal 17 November 17 1921
69. Irish News 19 December 1922

70. Eamon Phoenix – op.cit., p286
71. Eamon Phoenix – op.cit., p281
72. Brian Lacy – Siege City (Belfast 1980) p231
73. Eamon Phoenix – op.cit p322
74. Letter from Cahir Healy to the Editor of *Irish Statesman*
    18 December 1925 (PRONI D2991/13/9)

CONCLUSION

1.Maryan Valiulis – *Portrait of a Revolutionary, General Richard Mulcahy and the Founding of the Irish Free State.* p25
2 .D. G. Boyce (Ed.) – *The Revolution in Ireland. 1879-1923.* (Macmillan 1988) P48/49
3 D.G. Boyce (Ed.) – Op. cit., p54

Abbreviations

BNL	Belfast News Letter
DJ	Derry Journal
GAA	Gaelic Athletic Association
ICA	Irish Citizen Army
IRA	Irish Republican Army
IRB	Irish Republican Brotherhood
INV	Irish National Volunteers
ITGWU	Irish Transport & General Workers Union
IV	Irish Volunteers
RIC	Royal Irish Constabulary
RUC	Royal Ulster Constabulary
SF	Sinn Féin
UUC	Ulster Unionist Council
UVF	Ulster Volunteer Force

BIBLIOGRAPHY

PRIMARY SOURCES

Public Record Office of Northern Ireland. Belfast

Cahir Healy Papers. (D.2991)
Municipal Elections and PR (1914-26) (D.1074)
J. McCarroll Papers (T.2257)
Joe Devlin – T.24 24

Minutes and Correspondence of Derry Corporation

County Donegal Historical Society Museum
(Franciscan Friary, Rossnowlagh)
Liam O'Duffy Documents on IRA Activity (1920-21)

Reports (Microfilm held in Magee Library)
Dublin Castle Records – Colonial Office CO 904 – The British in Ireland
Part Four Police Reports. 1914-21
(CO.904 Boxes 92-122 and 148-156A)

NEWSPAPERS

Belfast News Letter
Derry Journal
Freeman's Journal
Irish News
Irish Press
Londonderry Sentinel

OFFICIAL PUBLICATIONS

Report of the Irish Boundary Commission 1925 – Introduction by Geoffrey
J. Hand (Shannon 1969)

SECONDARY SOURCES

Beckett, J C, *The Making of Modern Ireland 1603-1923.* (London1981)
Bowman, John, *De Valera and the Ulster Question 1917-73.* (Oxford 1982)
Boyce, D J (ed), *Revolution in Ireland 1879-1923.* (Dublin 1988)
Boyd, Andrew, *Holy War in Belfast.* (Belfast 1987)
Buckland, Patrick, *The Factory of Grievances 1921-39.* (Dublin 1979)
Connolly, James, *Labour in Ireland* (Dublin 1910)
Coogan, Tim Pat, *Michael Collins, A Biography.* (London 1990)
Curran, Frank, *Derry: Countdown to Disaster.* (Dublin 1986)
Dangerfield, George, *The Damnable Question.* (London 1977)
Doherty, Wm, *Derry Columbkille* (Adm. Long Tower). (Derry n.p. 1899)
Farrell, Michael, *Northern Ireland: The Orange State.* (London 1976)
Fitzpatrick, David, *Politics and Irish Life 1913-23.* (Dublin 1977)
Gallagher, Frank, *The Indivisable Island.* (London 1959)
Gailey, Andrew, *Ireland and the Death of Kindness.* (Cork 1987)
Greaves, C Desmond, *The Life and Times of James Connolly.* (London 1961)
Hand, G J, 'McNeill and the Boundary Commission' in Martin and F J Byrne
(eds), *The Scholar-Revolutionary Eoin McNeill 1867-1945.* (Shannon 1973)
Hogan, David, *Four Glorious Years.* (Dublin 1954)
Hughes, Sam, *City on the Foyle.* (Derry 1984)
Kee, Robert, *The Green Flag.* (London 1970)
Kennedy, Dennis, *The Widening Gulf.* (Belfast 1985)
Lacy, Brian, *Siege City.* (Belfast 1990)
Lee, Joseph, *Modernisation of Irish Society 1848-1918.* (Dublin 1973)
Loughlin, James, *Gladstone, Home Rule and the Ulster Question 1882-93.*
(Dublin 1986)
Lyons, F S L, *Ireland Since the Famine.* (Suffolk 1973)

Macardle, Dorothy, *The Irish Republic.* (London 1968)

McCann, Eamonn, *War and an Irish Town.* (London 1984)

McCartney, John F, *Pennyburn, An Historic Part of Derry City.* (Dublin 1984)

Murphy, Desmond *Derry, Donegal and Modern Ulster (1791-1921).* (Derry 1981)

O'Connor, Ulick, *Oliver St.John Gogarty.* (London 1981)

O'Faolin Sean, *The Irish 1948.* (Revised Paperback 1969)

O'Leary, Cornelius, *Irish Elections 1918-77.* (Dublin 1979)

Phoenix, Eamon, *Northern Nationalism.* (Belfast 1994)

Stewart, A T Q, *The Narrow Ground.* (London 1977)

Taylor, Rex, *Michael Collins.* (London 1958)

Tierney, Michael, *Eoin McNeill, Scholar & Man of Action 1867-1945.* (Oxford 1980)

Valuilis, Maryann, *Portrait of a Revolutionary, General Richard Mulcahy* (Dublin 1992)

THESIS

Eamon Phoenix, *The Nationalist Movement in Northern Ireland,* 1914-28 (Ph.D. Q.U.B. 1983)

INTERVIEWS

George Hamill

Ronald O'Doherty

Mrs Teresa Moore (nee Shiels)

Mrs Jean Donohue

Mr Leo Emerson

TELEVISION DOCUMENTARY

Marcus, Louis (dir.) "The Irish Condition" Radio Telefis Eireann 1994

INDEX